LITURGY AND MUSE

Liturgia condenda 14

1. Gerard Lukken & Mark Searle, *Semiotics and Church Architecture. Applying the Semiotics of A.J. Greimas and the Paris School to the Analysis of Church Buildings*, Kampen, 1993
2. Gerard Lukken, *Per visibilia ad invisibilia. Anthropological, Theological and Semiotic Studies on the Liturgy and the Sacraments*, edited by Louis van Tongeren & Charles Caspers, Kampen, 1994
3. *Bread of Heaven. Customs and Practices Surrounding Holy Communion. Essays in the History of Liturgy and Culture*, edited by Charles Caspers, Gerard Lukken & Gerard Rouwhorst, Kampen, 1995
4. Willem Marie Speelman, *The Generation of Meaning in Liturgical Songs. A Semiotic Analysis of Five Liturgical Songs as Syncretic Discourses*, Kampen, 1995
5. Susan K. Roll, *Toward the Origins of Christmas*, Kampen, 1995
6. Maurice B. McNamee, *Vested Angels. Eucharistic Allusions in Early Netherlandish Paintings*, Leuven, 1998
7. Karl Gerlach, *The Antenicene Pascha. A Rhetorical History*, Leuven, 1998
8. Paul Post, Jos Pieper & Marinus van Uden, *The Modern Pilgrim. Multidisciplinary Explorations of Christian Pilgrimage*, Leuven, 1998
9. Judith Marie Kubicki, *Liturgical Music as Ritual Symbol. A Case Study of Jacques Berthier's Taizé Music*, Leuven, 1999
10. Justin E.A. Kroesen, *The Sepulchrum Domini through the Ages. Its Form and Function*, Leuven, 2000
11. Louis van Tongeren, *Exaltation of the Cross. Toward the Origins of the Feast of the Cross and the Meaning of the Cross in Early Medieval Liturgy*, Leuven, 2000
12. P. Post, G. Rouwhorst, L. van Tongeren, A. Scheer (eds.), *Christian Feast and Festival. The Dynamics of Western Liturgy and Culture*, Leuven, 2001
13. V. Rosier, *Liturgical Catechesis of Sunday Celebrations in the Absence of a Priest*, Leuven, 2002

Liturgia condenda is published by the Liturgical Institute in Tilburg (NL). The series plans to publish innovative research into the science of liturgy and serves as a forum which will bring together publications produced by researchers of various nationalities. The motto *liturgia condenda* expresses the conviction that research into the various aspects of liturgy can make a critico-normative contribution to the deepening and the renewal of liturgical practice.

Liturgisch Instituut
P.O. Box 9130
5000 HC Tilburg, The Netherlands

LITURGY AND MUSE

The Eucharistic Prayer

A. Vernooij

PEETERS
LEUVEN - PARIS - DUDLEY, MA

Library of Congress Cataloging-in-Publication Data

Liturgy and muse: the Eucharistic prayer / A. Vernooij (ed.).
p. cm. -- (Liturgia condenda ; 14)
English and French.
Lectures delivered at a symposium held Oct. 13-14, 1999 at the University of Tilburg.
Includes bibliographical references and index.
ISBN 9042911751
I. Eucharistic prayers--Congresses. 2. Communion-service music--Congresses. I. Vernooij, Anton, 1940- II. Series.

BV825-54 .L58 2002
264'.36--dc21 2002068415

D. 2002/0602/96
ISBN 90-429-1175-1

CONTENTS

ANTON VERNOOIJ

PREFACE

This book comprises the lectures from the symposium "Liturgy and the language of the muses", held on October 13 and 14, 1999, in the Maranatha chapel of the Theological Faculty, Tilburg (TFT).[1] For this volume the various authors have revised, expanded and provided notes to accompany the texts they read those days. The symposium was organised by the Liturgical Institute, which is located at the TFT, and the Netherlands Institute for Church Music, Utrecht, to mark my departure as lecturer from the latter, and appointment as special Professor of Liturgical Music in Tilburg. Among its participants the symposium counted 113 liturgists, church musicians and clergy from Belgium, the Netherlands and Germany. Each day was introduced with a presentation of the theme, by Professor Paul Post and Dr. Louis van Tongeren, respectively. The texts of their remarks are likewise included in this book. Both days closed with a concert.

The symposium was devoted to contemporary musical components and forms of expression in our liturgical action, with special focus on the eucharistic prayer. This is very much a vital topic in the Netherlands at the moment, and furthermore is in line with my research and teaching responsibilities as special professor. In my inaugural lecture, "Music as liturgical sign",[2] given on October 19, 1998, in the auditorium of the Catholic University of Brabant (University of Tilburg), I described the celebration of liturgy as an artwork which takes place in time and space, and which does not present itself to us as a collection of separate, successive units of text and action, but as one united whole. Within this total event, only in the language of the muses can people express that which moves them at the depths of their being. The encounter with God addresses mankind through all the senses in combination. The muse is the principle medium for the encounter with God.

[1] The TFT is part of the University of Tilburg.

[2] Baarn 1998.

Translating the lectures into English presented several problems. The most important of these was how to deal with the texts of Dutch songs and poems which were cited, and which were difficult to translate into English. Sometimes the text was paraphrased. On several occasions it was decided to omit a poem, such as for instance one by Lucebert in the lecture by Huub Oosterhuis. The lecture by Joseph Gelineau has been included in French, the language in which it was delivered. A written rendering of this address, which was improvised with such verve at the time, was provided by A. Hollaardt, M.A., O.P. One contribution was omitted entirely, namely the introduction to and score of a sung eucharistic prayer which the composer Jos Beijer (b. 1970) wrote especially for the symposium, and which was performed and discussed on the second day.

In addition to the lectures from the symposium this book contains an extensive article, "Music and liturgy in movement", which I wrote at the request of colleagues. As it happens, they have many times asked for an English language overview of the history of Roman Catholic church music in the Netherlands, and particularly of the Amsterdam Study Group for Vernacular Liturgy, whose influence on liturgical music has reached beyond the borders of the Netherlands.

Particularly Dr. Charles Caspers, the former secretary of the Liturgical Institute, contributed substantially to the realisation of the symposium. I wish to express my warmest thanks to him, not only for having given fully of his great organisational talents in putting the extensive event together, but also for his editorial contribution toward this book coming to be. In this regard, I must also express my thanks no less to his successor, Dr. Els Rose. Publication was made possible in part by a grant from the Dutch St. Gregory Association, which provides direction for church music in the Netherlands, and is also the patron underwriting the special chair of Liturgical Music at the TFT. The contributions of Joosse, Oosterhuis, Post, Schuman, Van Tongeren and Vernooij were translated into English by D. Mader.

If the symposium, and the written record of the various lectures which now lies before you, contributes to further confirming liturgical music as a basic category of Christian ritual, I will regard myself as having fully succeeded in the intention of both undertakings.

Paul Post

"THE MILIEU OF THE MUSE": SOME INTRODUCTORY NOTES WITH REGARD TO THE THEME

I. Reactions

When word got around the Netherlands that a symposium on sung eucharistic prayer was being planned, in part by the inter-university Liturgical Institute at Tilburg, well before the distribution of a brochure and programme we were confronted with divergent reactions. Some – indeed, I must say most – displayed enthusiasm. They viewed the theme as appropriate, and vital. I suspect that this spontaneous reaction chiefly recognised and valued the dimension of the muse, and in particular music, as combined with the heart of ecclesiastical ritual. Here and there there was also an undertone of tension and expectancy. This is not a subject which can be approached and handled non-committally and with academic detachment: it touches pastoral-liturgical practice, and the questions and disappointments, the challenges and perspectives that hold sway there.

There was also another reaction, which, to be honest, I had absolutely not expected. Some expressed concern about our plans. Was such a conference on eucharistic prayer really wise, now? Several indicated that they would not come, despite their interest. Because of their ecclesiastical/liturgical responsibilities it was better that they kept their distance. The lectures were going to be printed and they could order a copy? Gladly!

Initially this reaction – and I am certainly not dramatising it in order to suggest that we are really somewhere out on the front lines of liturgy and liturgical studies – surprised me. It was also hard to identify what was causing the anxiety. Later I caught sight of the underlying motives. People supposed that the symposium would be about eucharistic prayer in the Netherlands, the complex interaction of sanctioned and unsanctioned eucharistic prayers, the good and bad in the liturgical double project of the 1970s.[1] Yes, perhaps new, unsanctioned

[1] H. Wegman (ed.): *Goed of niet goed? Het eucharistisch gebed in Nederland*, 1-2 (Hilversum 1976-1978); the second volume was presented as a Festschrift to Prof.dr. H. Manders.

eucharistic prayers would even receive the Great Seal from prominent liturgists there, just now that it had become somewhat quieter on this pastoral-liturgical front. When I encountered the concern expressed in this way, I could understand this reaction a little better.

2. The theme

With these reactions in mind, and particularly taking into account the latter noises of concern, it is well to further locate the theme of the symposium and of this collection.

I can begin with a reassurance, or, depending on one's starting point, by dispelling an illusion: the theme does not involve eucharistic prayer *an sich*, sanctioned or not. We are embarked for an entirely different, and to my mind much more important and fundamental pastoral-liturgical front in liturgical studies. It follows from the rather general interest, or the interest which has already arisen, in the fundamental, anthropological, symbolic-ritual dimensions of liturgy.[2] It also naturally follows from the appointment of Anton Vernooij holding the special chair for liturgical music at the Theological Faculty Tilburg, and from his inaugural lecture on the general principle of music as symbol,[3] regarding liturgy and *artes*, music, the discourse of the muse as a defining and sustaining dimension of liturgical action. The dimension of the muse is the theme of this volume, with eucharistic prayer as the case study. This perspective, reflected in various ways throughout this collection, is thus what directs our discussion of eucharistic prayer. Following this general positioning of the theme, I wish to place it in a broader context.

3. The theme is 'in'

First of all, it is no exaggeration to say that our theme, our double theme of the discourse of the muse and eucharistic prayer, is 'in', is vital,

[2] G. Lukken: *Rituelen in overvloed. Een kritische bezinning op de plaats en de gestalte van het christelijk ritueel in onze cultuur* (Baarn 1999); M. Barnard & P. Post (eds.): *Ritueel bestek. Antropologische kernwoorden van de liturgie* (Zoetermeer 2001).

[3] A. Vernooij: *Muziek als liturgisch teken. Rede (...) bij de aanvaarding van het ambt van bijzonder hoogleraar liturgische muziek aan de Theologische Faculteit Tilburg* (Baarn/Heeswijk-Dinther 1998) (= Liturgie in perspectief 10).

is blowing in the wind, as one might put it. For instance, recently there were several important congresses on eucharistic prayer. I am particularly thinking of the gathering at Sant'Anselmo in Rome, the proceedings of which were published not long ago in a thick issue of *Ecclesia orans*.[4] Mainly, though, I have in mind the scores of conferences, books and collections devoted to liturgy and music, to the artistic-liturgical dimension, or however they may name or refer to it. In that company I would list the Finnish conference on liturgical music of the Societas Liturgica, the proceedings of which appeared in a special issue of *Studia Liturgica*;[5] and especially a recent issue of the Northern Italian *Rivista Liturgica* on 'L'In-canto del rito', where the theme is dealt with in the example of the *prex eucharistica*.[6] In that fine issue there are, for the rest, a number of prominent Italian liturgists who speak out candidly on, among other things, the artistic dimensions of the eucharistic prayer. It strikes me how in the Northern Italian sphere there are hardly any traces to be found of the concern and reservations about touching on this theme we noted in the introduction. Liturgists like Sabaino, Rainoldi and Costa on the one hand reflect forthrightly, creatively and

[4] *The eucharistic prayer. Theology and practice* (Rome 1999) (= Ecclesia Orans 16,2). In this, see P. MARINI: La riforma della preghiera eucaristica dopo il concilio 163-168; E. LA VERDIERE: The Eucharist in the New Testament. Approaches and perspectives 169-188; P. DE CLERCK: Les épiclèses des nouvelles prières eucharistiques du rite romain. Leur importance théologique 189-208; D. POWER: The sacramental language of the eucharistic prayer 209- 232; E. MAZZA: L'anafora eucaristica e il problema della consacrazione. Alcuni dati della teologia medievale 233-282; C. GIRAUDO: L'eucologia anaforica tra istanze di inculturazione e fedeltà alla tradizione. Per una crescita del "depositum ecclesiae orantis" 299-324; J. CASTELLANO CERVERA: Relazione di sintesi sul Colloquium on the eucharistic prayer 325-342.

[5] *Societas Liturgica 1997 Turku Congress Liturgy and Music* (London 1998) (= Studia Liturgica 28,1). In this, chiefly I. PAHL: Music and liturgical celebration. Presidential Adress 1-13; Ph. HARNONCOURT: The anthropological and liturgical-theological foundations of music in worship 14-31.

[6] *L'In-canto del rito* (Padova 1999) (= Rivista Liturgica 86,2-3). In this, chiefly D. SAIBANO: Musica e liturgia. Dalla 'Sacrosanctum concilium' al 'Repertorio nazionale dei canti liturgici'. Per una rilettura musicologico-liturgica di documenti ufficiali e 'Praenotanda' 173-198; E. COSTA: Produzione e appropriazione. Contesti, intermediari, condizionamenti 199-210; P. RIMOLDI: Parole e musica. Problemi e prospettive del rapporto tra liturgia e 'arti del suono' 211-223; F. RAINOLDI: I testi liturgici nei diversi contesti celebrativi. Testi e contesti 225-245; M. VEUTHEY: La preghiera eucaristica 309-320; J.-C. CRIVELLI: La salmodia e i suoi versetti 321-338; C. VALENZIANO: Nuova musica per la liturgia 343-348.

objectively on liturgical material, and on the other hand are involved in putting together much of the approved papal liturgy, such as the liturgy designed for the Jubilee year in 2000, and the commemoration of, for instance, Little Teresia.[7]

In a more general sense we can also point to the great interest in the expressive, artistic dimension, for the *artes*, in ecclesiastical and theological circles.[8] In the adoption of sung eucharistic prayer as our case study for the artistic dimension of liturgical acts, we are in the midst of a popular current. Unavoidably, the question must arise of whether that is a good thing. It is easy to create the impression that we are eager to swim along with a stream of fashions and trends. It can also be asked how deep and abiding that interest for the *artes* in the Church and theology is, and whether it is not, for instance, chiefly the context of aestheticising and musealising that drives the interest. Whatever the case, the trend is inescapably there. That is proven by the flood of lectures, books, workshops etc., that are devoted to themes from the realm of the Church and art. It has a voice in the recent pastoral letter of the pope to all artists.[9] Further evidence is found in the fact that in 'Liturgia condenda', the international series from our Liturgical Institute, of the thirteen volumes that have appeared to date at least five deal explicitly with subjects from the realm of liturgy and *artes*: two on church architecture, one on painting, two on church music.[10] I also find the fact significant, to mention another current signal, that at the symposium in honour of the 85th birthday of the theologian Edward Schillebeeckx in November, 1999, it was hardly theologians, with their classical systematic/theological discourse, who were in the limelight, but rather artistic

[7] See the literature listed in the preceding note.

[8] It is both unfeasible, and to my mind unnecessary, to illustrate this with examples; see the survey of literature in P. POST (ed.): *Een ander huis. Kerkarchitectuur na 2000* (Baarn/Heeswijk-Dinther 1997) (= Liturgie in perspectief 7) 96-101.

[9] *Brief von Papst Johannes Paul II. An die Künstler* (Vatican City 1999).

[10] G. LUKKEN & M. SEARLE: *Semiotics and church architecture. Applying the semiotics of A.J. Greimas and the Paris School to the analysis of church buildings* (Kampen 1993) (= Liturgia condenda 1); M.B. MCNAMEE: *Vested angels. Eucharistic allusions in early Netherlandish paintings* (Leuven 1998) (= Liturgia condenda 6); W.M. SPEELMAN: *The generation of meaning in liturgical songs. A semiotic analysis of five liturgical songs as syncretic discourses* (Kampen 1995) (= Liturgia condenda 4); J.M. KUBICKI: *Liturgical music as ritual symbol. A case study of Jacques Berthier's Taizé music* (Leuven 1999) (= Liturgia condenda 9); J. KROESEN: *The Sepulchrum Domini through the ages. Its form and function.* (Leuven 2000) (= Liturgia condenda 10).

sources, modern art, contemporary pop music, film and literature. That should give one pause, particularly if one reflects on the special issue of the *Tijdschrift voor theologie* that appeared in honour of the same Schillebeeckx 25 years ago on his 60th birthday. Then that issue contained, aside from a short word from the Dutch poet Gabriel Smit (1910-1981) and an artistic travel impression with drawings, only one other contribution with any orientation to the muses, and at that one which was then held in a certain disdain: an article by L. Meulenberg (b. 1936) on the expressive narrative discourse of the folk tale.[11] Times change.

But let us count our blessings: our theme is 'in', we find ourselves on a cutting edge in Church and theology. Among the advantages of this is that we have conversation partners, credentials even, that we are not isolated off in a corner practising a hobby of which the broader ecclesiastical, theological and cultural relevance can only be explained with difficulty.

Yet I think it is of importance, within that whole of fashion and trends, to see and to search for that which is specific to liturgy and liturgical studies in the artistic perspective. With a certain arrogance we could, after all, say that that perspective is linked with liturgy and liturgical studies in a more insistent way than it is with anything else. I will work that out briefly later.

4. Integral, contextual approach

This essential – thus neither chance nor merely stylish – attention for the artistic dimension hangs together closely with the development that liturgical studies have undergone in the twentieth century. In any case, it must be acknowledged that for a long time there was an extremely limited view of the liturgical object. Liturgical studies focused on liturgical books, and at that chiefly on the rubrics. Accordingly it was an extremely practical and normative discipline that was generally housed at seminaries along with church law, or taught by the most practical figure on the

[11] T.M. Schoof (ed.): *De positie van de theoloog. Sonderingen voor Schillebeeckx* (Utrecht 1974) (= Tijdschrift voor theologie 14,4). In this: L. Meulenberg: Theologie. Pleidooi voor het sprookje 357-364.

staff, the bursar, who also was responsible for the lodgings, potatoes, wine and cigars. For the rest, however, he was not always the most artistic person on the faculty. To an important extent, study consisted of becoming acquainted with the book and the rubric, and subsequently mastering them.

Now, in the context of the Liturgical Movement there came a growing realisation of 'liturgy beyond texts'. An integral approach to the liturgical object came to be generally acknowledged by members of the discipline. The narrow conception of liturgy broadened out spectacularly. In the definition used by the Dutch national research programme in liturgical studies, liturgy includes "all symbolic action with which Christian communities express their faith".[12] That expression comprises a very extensive repertoire of human action: gestures, body movements, music, visual imagery, words, texts. Anything could be a valuable source, and its study demanded considerable skill – certainly more methods and techniques than those from literary/historical quarters alone. The discipline underwent what has been called its *anthropologische Wende*. The conviction grew that one had to take seriously the general/human aspects in regard to the ritual act. Thus scholars began to reflect on ritual and symbol, language and act, on the sensory and the physical, on verbal and non-verbal elements. Each of these anthropological/ritual dimensions brought with it the necessity of specialised expertise, with a series of new alliances, methods and techniques. Thus by now in liturgical studies there is unavoidably a continual mutual dynamic interaction among new sources, new methods and techniques, new questions and new alliances and partners within the academic sphere.

Cohering with this integral approach to liturgy, context has come to receive abundant attention. Unavoidably people began to see the multiple contextualities. In the broader ritual-liturgical framework of liturgical renewal, the fundamental realisation grew that liturgical studies had to take seriously not only the general basic human aspects in regard to ritual acts, but also the complex cultural and anthropological context.

[12] For the most recent survey of this programme, see P. POST: Liturgische Bewegungen und Festkultur. Ein landesweites liturgiewissenschaftliches Forschungsprogramm in den Niederlanden, in *Liturgisches Jahrbuch* 48 (1998) 96-113. See also the outcome of this programme, which appeared as P. POST et al. (eds.): *Christian feast and festival. The dynamics of Western liturgy and culture* (Leuven 2001) (= Liturgia condenda 12).

It was realised that every liturgical study was an anthropological as well as a cultural study. To the necessity for a general integral approach to the liturgical object, there was now added the consciousness of the necessity for a broad, contextual research project. It must be noted, while on the topic of this broad context of the integral and contextual approach to liturgy, that it would not be long before we encountered the *artes* there, and within them the discourse of the muse.

It remains difficult to fully do justice to the breadth of the implications of these notions for liturgy and liturgical studies. Music is not just a formal question; it is not just a matter of packaging, adding to or detracting from the contents; no, it involves an integrated dimension of the liturgical symbolic act. Yet to a certain extent music also is and remains an independent source, a peculiar *source liturgique*.

In a lecture given at the conference referred to above on liturgy and music at the Societas Liturgica, Philipp Harnoncourt (b. 1931) referred to neurophysical brain research.[13] It has been shown that people with damage to the cortex can no longer work with texts, cannot speak and cannot remember texts they have heard or read. But if one links the text with music, and the same person sings or listens to them, the situation changes: they can speak by singing; sung texts can be remembered. Recited or sung text material is stored somewhere else in the brain, in a different place. I find that a fascinating discovery which I would connect with the observation that coma patients prefer to be brought back to consciousness by poetry and music.

5. Research design

In this connection I would also want to refer to another not unimportant aspect of the *artes* being on the agenda of our discipline. Today, more than before, people have an eye for the role that the *artes* can fulfil in a research model (also called the 'research design') in theology in general, and liturgical studies in particular. While on the one hand people search for and work with 'hard' methods and techniques, I also see a growing interest in 'softer' methods of research. This 'softer' line works

[13] HARNONCOURT: The anthropological and liturgical-theological foundations 19.

rather with narrative, visual, aesthetic, artistic or experience-oriented discourses. It is not my purpose to play the 'hard' and 'soft' research traditions against one another, as does occasionally happen; neither is it my purpose to propagate the 'soft' line all the way out into its impressionistic and primary-intuitive-associative, unverifiable disciplinary exercise. It is my purpose though to reveal the role that the *artes* can play in the research model. Thus, I see, for instance, the important role of what is termed 'tamed intuition', nourished and actuated by narrative and images, in the liturgical studies research design of liturgists such as Herman Wegman (1930-1996) and Gerard Lukken (b. 1933).[14] The *artes*, after all, enter into things naturally through the integral source which is a primary and irreplaceable source for us. If the dimension of the muse is an inseparable part of any liturgical symbolic act, then this dimension inevitably comes back in the study of and 'opening up' of the source, with all the consequences that will have. I think we still have too little overview of the consequences of this, are still inclined in study and teaching to present the liturgical source as text. I suddenly became aware of this during a guest lecture in Tilburg in 1998. Prof. Nico Botha, from Pretoria, South Africa, was lecturing on funeral rituals in the South African coloured township of Eersterust. He was presenting the ritual, when suddenly his lecture switched (he still properly at the rostrum, we in rows in our seats, pens at the ready) into loud singing, clapping and dancing, a for him self-evident and appropriate presentation of the liturgical repertoire of the funeral ceremony. Now, our reaction, and not his singing, clapping and dancing, is the point: we looked at one another, surprised and a bit uncomfortable. What were we supposed to think of this? Where was this going to go from there? That reaction speaks volumes – just as slide presentations, poems and music still remain too much the exception in our lecture halls.

6. Inculturation

I still want to mention explicitly the sustaining perspective of inculturation, which ultimately colours our theme.[15] By discussing together, and

[14] Cf. P. Post: Feast as a key concept in a liturgical studies research design, in Post et al. (eds.): *Christian feast and festival* 47-77; Idem: Interference and intuition: on the characteristic nature of research design in liturgical studies, in *Questions liturgiques / Studies in Liturgy* 81 (2000) 48-65.

[15] For the boom in literature on liturgical inculturation, I would first of all list the survey by G. Lukken: Inculturatie van de liturgie. Theorie en praktijk, in J. Lamberts

making music together, we would explore the possible connections of liturgical play with the surrounding culture, or, rather, cultures. Precisely at the level of the *artes*, at that of the discourse of the muse in particular, great opportunities await us. It is, I am convinced, necessary to sound and sample the actual symbolic order constantly. As is increasingly being acknowledged, this order is at its deepest defined by images, music, spatial order and physicality. And, on the other hand, sounding and sampling of the symbolic milieu via image and music is unusually productive: via these symbolic-ritual dimensions one penetrates most deeply into a culture. The domain is rich and wide: football supporters in stadiums, housemusic, Gregorian chant at festivals, TV shows and pop musicals. This is done not to mindlessly embrace them as inculturating forms for our liturgy, but certainly as the necessary preparatory phase for the double movement of liturgical inculturation, viz. to let, on the one side, our liturgical play be amenable to the culture surrounding it, and on the other to let the surrounding culture be amenable to the gospel and expression of faith in liturgical act.

7. Feast and connection

Finally, I would return once again to liturgy, music and eucharistic prayer. What strikes me in the literature on our double theme which is momentarily so amply available is how two aspects are almost generally elucidated.[16] The first is the element of feast, of festivity: music

(ed.): *Liturgie en inculturatie* (Leuven/Amersfoort 1996) (= Nikè-reeks 37) 15-56 = G. Lukken: Inculturation de la liturgie. Théorie et pratique, in *Questions liturgiques / Studies in Liturgy* 77 (1996) 1-39. This survey can be supplemented by S.A. Stauffer: Worship and culture. A select bibliography, in *Studia Liturgica* 27 (1997) 102-128; Lutheran World Federation. Chicago Statement on worship and culture: baptism and rites of passage, in *Studia Liturgica* 28,2 (1998) 244-252; A.M. Triacca & A. Pistoia (eds.): *Liturgie et cultures* (Rome 1997) (= Bibliotheca Ephemerides Liturgicae 90); A.M. Triacca: 'Inculturazione e liturgia'. Eventi dello Spirito Santo. A proposito di alcuni principi per il progresso dell'approfonimento degli studi su 'liturgia e cultura', in *Ecclesia Orans* 15,1 (1998) 59-90; H. Bauernfeind: *Inkulturation der Liturgie in unsere Gesellschaft. Eine Kriteriensuche, aufgezeigt an den Zeitzeichen Kirche heute, Esoterik/New Age und modernes Menschsein* (Würzburg 1998) (= Studien zur Theologie und Praxis der Seelsorge 34); Lukken: *Rituelen in overvloed* 122-143.

[16] See particularly the previously mentioned conference of the Societas Liturgica (note 5 above) and the special issue of *Rivista Liturgica* (note 6 above).

internalises feast, music elevates liturgy to feast.[17] Second, there is the integrating dimension of music. This quality has been noted and lauded from various perspectives.[18] Every liturgy is an arrangement, an eclectic project, a collection of often highly varied elements. Liturgy appears to have been a postmodern artistic project *avant la lettre*; time and again bits and pieces were lifted from their primary contexts and assembled into a new project. Every liturgical arrangement is thus complex, a construction of extremely diverse materials with divergent functions and origins. Parts come from home liturgy, parts from court or papal liturgy, parts bear the colours of the early Church or its Jewish forebears, other parts are medieval, some are redolent of the sphere of the East, others of the West. Liturgy is thus a work, a *poièma* with the character of a montage, which can only exist by grace of a connection, a connection which holds the whole together, homogenises it and makes it into a new entity. The eucharistic prayer is a striking example of such a montage. Certainly eight distinct genres (thanksgiving, acclamation, epiclesis, institution narrative and consecration, anamnesis, oblatio, prayer of intercession and closing doxology) form one whole. It is pre-eminently music that can contribute to connection among the pieces. In addition to the festive dimension, there is thus the integrative dimension of music in liturgy.

[17] As was one of the main notions of the Dutch national research programme on Christian feast and festival; see note 12, above.

[18] See, for instance, RAINOLDI: I testi liturgici 233.

Gerard Rouwhorst

THE DESIGN OF SUNG EUCHARISTIC PRAYER IN THE TRADITION

1. Introduction

The conviction that analysis of liturgical rituals should not be limited to the description and interpretation of the content of texts has won ever more territory in liturgical studies over the past decades. Thanks to the influence of disciplines such as social and cultural anthropology, semiotics, what are termed "ritual studies", linguistics and the studies which are occupied with interpersonal communication, researchers have obtained more insight into the non-verbal elements that play an essential role in rituals, such as the use of space and, not least, the delivery of a ritual text. This latter means that it is not only important to know *what* is in a liturgical text, but also *how* it is performed. Is a text read, recited or sung? What rules apply to its performance? What role do rhythm and intonation play in it? If it is sung, what melodies are used? How does the manner of speaking, reciting, singing, etc. relate to everyday ways of speaking or singing? Subsequently, it is also important to know who delivers the text. Is it done by a formal worship leader, a priest, or primarily by the community? And to what degree is there interaction between the celebrant and the community?

There are few liturgical historians today who will deny that questions of this sort are of essential importance for the study of the history of the eucharistic prayer. At the same time it must be acknowledged that it is far from easy for liturgical historians to form for themselves a reasonably sound image of the practice surrounding the performance of that prayer in the past, that is to say, not only of the content of the texts of eucharistic prayers, but also the liturgical setting in which they functioned and the manner in which they were spoken, declaimed, or perhaps sung. There is little about this aspect of the eucharistic prayer to be found in the sources available to us. Anyone opening an edition of the Missal from 1970, for instance, will find there nothing more than a number of recitation settings for the various prefaces, for the institution narrative and the anamnesis, and for the closing doxology, and further a melody for several other parts of Eucharistic Prayer I (the Roman Canon). In the Roman Missal of 1570 and also in the official books of most other Western and Eastern rites, we find even less, were that possible, at least if we leave out of consideration certain acclamations and songs that are sung by the community (the "people"), but which have a relatively loose connection with the eucharistic prayer itself. All this could perhaps be the explanation for the fact that in the literature – for instance, the various manuals in the field of liturgical and music history – extremely little is to be found on this matter, and most liturgical and music historians appear to give this subject a wide berth.

In spite of all this, I believe that it must still be possible to sketch, at least in broad outlines, a global picture of the historical development of the delivery of the eucharistic prayer, and also of its musical design. A condition for doing this is certainly that in addition to the "direct" method that involves study of sources in which explicit mention is made of the delivery of the eucharistic prayer, we dare to make use of a more indirect method. By this I mean that we must first of all try to form an image of the development of the eucharistic prayer in the past and of the ritual setting in which it functioned, and subsequently draw a number of conclusions regarding the manner of delivery, for example about the degree to which song would have played a role. The text itself, and the setting in which it is spoken, can in some cases have indeed contributed to the manner of delivery for the eucharistic prayer being differentiated from ordinary, everyday speech patterns, and developing in the direction of solemn declamation or a particular form of song – or in other cases, on the contrary, have precluded such development.

2. Points of departure

In my attempt to reconstruct the development of the delivery and the musical design of the eucharistic prayer, in addition to the method just sketched I will employ two other points of departure which I wish to make explicit before beginning.

(1) In liturgical history there are a number of fissures, at which, as it were, certain switches are located, and the train moves from its old track to a new one. With regard to the history of the eucharistic

prayer and musical design, one can distinguish two such fissures that have been of crucial importance: a) the fourth/fifth century, the period in which Christianity achieved public recognition and in a rather short time even became the state religion, and b) the transition from late antiquity to the Middle Ages, which particularly for Western liturgical history,[1] but also for its Eastern counterpart,[2] in many respects forms the beginning of a new period from the perspective of liturgy.

(2) To the extent that publications have appeared on the musical design of the eucharistic prayer,[3] as a rule these are almost exclusively concerned with the Western, Latin tradition. That is in itself understandable, but can also easily lead to a somewhat one-sided vision of the development in the past. It may be enlightening to compare the choices which were made in the West with developments that have taken place elsewhere – that is to say, in the East. This is of course not a matter of presenting an encyclopedic image, as complete as possible, of all the musical forms that we encounter in the history of eucharistic prayer, but rather a matter of getting an overview of the problems that have presented themselves with respect to the design of the eucharistic prayer, and of the solutions which have been chosen for them. Insight into this matter relativises one's own tradition. Moreover, in principle there is a possibility that people elsewhere have found solutions which have been overlooked in one's own tradition – and even if this is not the case, it will become clearer how difficult the problems were with which people were confronted.

[1] Cf. A. ANGENENDT: *Geschichte der Religiosität im Mittelalter* (Darmstadt 1997), esp. 351-515.

[2] The idea that Eastern liturgies developed much less than their Western counterparts since antiquity is decidedly inaccurate. In this connection, see the succinct and informative introduction to the history of Byzantine liturgy of R. TAFT: *The Byzantine Rite. A short history* (Collegeville 1992).

[3] See especially M. ROBERT: Le Canon devrait-il être chanté? in *Revue grégorienne* 42 (1964) 84-90; J. CLAIRE: Deux mélodies pour le chant du Canon, in *Revue grégorienne* 42 (1964) 91-101; A. GERHARDS: Höhepunkt auf dem Tiefpunkt? Überlegungen zur musikalischen Gestalt des eucharistischen Hochgebets, in E. RENHART & A. SCHNIDER (eds.): *Sursum corda. Variationen zu einem liturgischen Motiv. Für Philipp Harnoncourt zum 60. Geburtstag* (Graz 1991) 167-177; J. GELINEAU: New models for the eucharistic prayer as praise of all the assembly, in *Studia Liturgica* 27 (1997) 79-87.

The arrangement of this contribution is already roughly indicated by these points. It will consist of three sections: a) the eucharistic prayer and its possible musical design in the period prior to Constantine; b) the eucharistic prayer and its possible musical design from that date into late antiquity, both in the West and the East; c) the development from the Middle Ages until the 20th and 21st centuries, in East and West.

3. THE PERIOD BEFORE CONSTANTINE

3.1. Composition

Until recently people had a rather clear picture of the eucharistic prayer in the first centuries of Christianity. They proceeded from the assumption that there were various traditions on this point, as was also the case in a later period, for instance in the fourth century, the era of the classic Western and Eastern anaphoras, but at the same time they proceeded from the assumption that there existed a generally accepted basic structure in which a number of constantly recurring elements had a fixed place. It was generally assumed in the past decades that this basic structure was derived from the *birkat ha-mazon*, the thanksgiving that the Jews pronounced after meals. This basic structure of the early Christian eucharistic prayer was further supposed to be characterised by a tripartite division. For instance, in his manual of liturgical history and in various other publications, Herman Wegman distinguished three strophes: a) an expression of praise directed to the Name of God; b) a memorial and thanksgiving to God for Jesus Christ; and c) a petition for the coming of the Holy Spirit.[4] Next, as a rule it was assumed that at a very early stage a version of the narrative of institution was inserted somewhere in the prayer.[5] That could have happened at various places, and

[4] H. WEGMAN: *Riten en mythen. Liturgie in de geschiedenis van het christendom* (Kampen 1991) 87, 155-156. See also IDEM: Genealogie des Eucharistiegebetes, in *Archiv für Liturgiewissenschaft* 33 (1991) 193-216 and G. ROUWHORST : Les oraisons de la table dans le Judaïsme et les célébrations eucharistiques des chrétiens syriaques, in *Questions liturgiques* 61 (1980) 211-240.

[5] See for instance the classic studies of G. DIX: *The shape of the liturgy* (London, 1945, 1978^{11}), esp. 214-237; J. JUNGMANN: *Missarum sollemnia* (Vienna 1952^{3}), esp. vol. I, 20-22.

that would explain why the various Eastern and Western eucharistic prayers differ considerably from one another with regard to structure.[6] Despite all the variations and differences, there would thus have still been one common pattern.

In the past ten to twenty years there have been increasing numbers of questions raised about this reconstruction. To begin with, the earlier assumption that it was simply to be accepted as a matter of fact that since Paul wrote his first letter to the Corinthians all Christian eucharistic prayers included an institution narrative, has completely disappeared among liturgical historians. That happened when scholars increasingly became aware of the fact that there are many eucharistic texts from the first four centuries which lack any trace of an institution narrative. One must mention the *Didache* in this connection, but also the old version of the Egyptian Markan anaphora, the Syrian anaphora of Addai and Mari, the eucharistic prayers from the Acts of Thomas, and the anaphora that forms the basis of the mystagogic catechesis of Cyril of Jerusalem.[7]

Ultimately, it appears that with further insight into the period before Constantine, only one single eucharistic prayer has been preserved for which it is absolutely certain that it contained the institution narrative: the eucharistic prayer that we encounter in what is termed the *Traditio Apostolica*,[8] which was the model for a number of the new eucharistic prayers in the second half of the twentieth century that were introduced by various churches. But that immediately raises the next problem. Until recently it was generally assumed that this text had come from a certain Hippolytus, a Roman bishop from the beginning of the third century. This view was particularly defended by Bernard Botte,[9] who did

[6] See especially L. LIGIER: De la Cène de Jésus à l'anaphore de l'Église, in *La Maison-Dieu* 87 (1966) 7-49; IDEM: The origins of the eucharistic prayer. From the Last Supper to the Eucharist, in *Studia Liturgica* 9 (1973) 161-185.

[7] For more precise references and further information, see G. ROUWHORST, La célébration de l'eucharistie dans l'église primitive, in *Questions liturgiques* 74 (1993) 89-112, p. 101-106; IDEM: De viering van de eucharistie in de vroege kerk, in *Tijdschrift voor Liturgie* 77 (1993) 207-222, p. 216-217. See also A. VERHEUL: La valeur consécratoire de la prière eucharistique, in *Studia Liturgica* 17 (1987) 221-231.

[8] B. BOTTE (ed.): *La Tradition apostolique de Saint Hippolyte. Essai de reconstitution* (Münster 1989[5]) (= Liturgiewissenschaftliche Quellen und Forschungen 39) 12-17.

[9] See particularly BOTTE: *La Tradition apostolique* xi-xix.

this with so much self-assurance, not to say bravura, that for a long time few appeared to have the courage to cast doubt on his thesis.[10] At the moment, however, it is being widely challenged. Everything that has to do with the person of Hippolytus and with the works that are attributed to him is again in question. That is also the case for the *Traditio Apostolica*. That it was written by Hippolytus – whoever he may have been – is now being called into doubt by many authors, and indeed it is now being questioned whether the document is not possibly of a later date.[11] With respect to the eucharistic prayer, it is important to note that in a recent publication on the prayer, the liturgical historian Bradshaw has advanced the hypothesis that while it is true that the prayer contains old layers that go back to the third century, this old core underwent a radical revision in the fourth century, and that only then was the institution narrative and the anamnesis which follows it included in the text.[12] Whether this hypothesis can be firmly established appears dubious to me. But even if that does not happen, one cannot deny that there are many indications that point to the institution narrative having been given a definite place in the eucharistic prayer at a rather late date. Perhaps we must here think even of the fourth century rather than the third.[13]

[10] One of the few exceptions was P. Nautin, who throughout his career disputed Botte's hypothesis. See particularly his work *Hippolyte et Josippe* (Paris 1947). Nautin's in certain respects laboured hypotheses were in turn contested by Botte, see for instance BOTTE: *La Tradition apostolique* xv-xvi.

[11] For the discussion with regard to this matter, see particularly M. METZGER: Nouvelles perspectives pour la prétendue *Tradition apostolique*, in *Ecclesia orans* 5 (1988) 241-259; IDEM: Enquêtes autour de la prétendue "Tradition apostolique", in *Ecclesia orans* 9 (1992) 7-36; P. BRADSHAW: Redating the Apostolic Tradition: some preliminary steps, in J. BALDOVIN & N. MITCHELL (eds.), *Rule of Prayer, Rule of Faith: essays in honor of Aidan Kavanagh* (Collegeville 1996) 3-17; C. MARKSCHIES: Wer schrieb die sogenannte *Traditio apostolica*?, in W. KINZIG, C. MARKSCHIES & M. VINZENT: *Tauffragen und Bekenntnis. Studien zur sogenannten "Traditio Apostolica", zu den "Interrogationes de fide" und zum "Römischen Glaubensbekenntnis"* (Berlin/New York 1999) 1-74. See also the papers of different (mainly Italian) authors published in *Ricerche su Ippolito* (Rome 1977) (= Studia Ephemeridis "Augustinianum" 13).

[12] P. BRADSHAW: The evolution of early anaphoras, in IDEM (ed.): *Essays on early Eastern eucharistic prayers* (Collegeville 1997) 1-18, p. 10-14.

[13] Thus BRADSHAW: The evolution 13-14. The fact that the institution narrative only received a place in the eucharistic prayer at a rather late date does not mean, however, that the tradition of Jesus's final meal did not play a crucial role in the development of the Christian celebration of the Eucharist. It undeniably did do so. Further, it is certainly not inconceivable that on specific occasions – one might think here particularly

Apart from the question of the institution narrative, recently questions have also been posed regarding the view that the eucharistic prayers from the first Christian centuries all proceeded according to a fixed pattern, and that they all preserved the tripartite structure of the *birkat ha-mazon*, for instance. P. Bradshaw, mentioned above, assumes a much greater diversity of traditions, forms and types of prayer.[14] Some texts would indeed have had a tripartite structure. But there would also perhaps have been prayers which were nothing more than an elaborate expression of praise, comparable with the *berachoth*, the short Jewish blessing that was pronounced before one ate bread, drank wine, or partook of other forms of food and drink. In this connection, P. Bradshaw also mentions the eucharistic prayers from the Apocryphal Acts of the Apostles, which have the character of a litany-like invocation of the Spirit or the Name.[15] It can be asked if Bradshaw does not somewhat too strongly stress the multiformity and perhaps gives a somewhat too disjointed picture of the eucharistic prayer in the first three Christian centuries. Personally I still find it plausible that the roots of the eucharistic prayer must primarily be sought in the Jewish thanksgiving after the meal, as Herman Wegman (among others) thought; but Bradshaw's reproach that many liturgists wrongly proceed from the assumption of great uniformity in and great continuity between the first/second and fourth centuries is, in my view, certainly correct.

Another item which is of importance here, and which is closely related to the previous, is that in the first centuries the texts of the eucharistic prayers were not yet fixed, and that at this point there was certainly room for improvisation. We must first note here that the texts of the Jewish prayers were not fixed. At this moment scholars are in rather general agreement that there is no sense in attempting to reconstruct the Ur-text of the *birkat ha-mazon*, for the simple reason that

of the Christian paschal celebration – it was certainly read. In this connection, compare ROUWHORST: L'Eucharistie 106-111.

[14] BRADSHAW: The evolution 10.

[15] For these prayers, see G. ROUWHORST: La célébration de l'Eucharistie selon les Actes de Thomas, in Ch. CASPERS & M. SCHNEIDERS: *Omnes circumadstantes. Contributions towards a history of the role of the people in the liturgy. Presented to Herman Wegman* (Kampen 1990) 51-77; C. JOHNSON: Ritual Epicleses in the Greek *Acts of Thomas*, in F. BOVON, A. BROCK & C.R. MATHEWS (eds.): *The Apocryphal Acts of the Apostles* (Cambridge Mass. 1999) (Harvard Divinity School Studies) 171-204.

such never existed.[16] There were various versions in circulation, and moreover there must have been room for improvisation. This must have been all the more true for the Christians who took over the model of the *birkat ha-mazon* in one form or another (assuming that is indeed what happened). The Jewish liturgical traditions that they for the most part preserved were not as such normative for them. They must have quite quickly begun to adapt them rather freely. Moreover, the texts of the prayers were, as a rule, not committed to writing, any more than were their Jewish counterparts, for that matter. All this explains the multiformity to which Bradshaw and others have pointed. But even when there was a prescribed framework or model, as in the case of the *Traditio Apostolica*, and even when a text was written down – which must have happened only very rarely before the fourth century – there was considerable space left for improvisation.[17]

3.2. Musical design

What, then, was the situation with regard to the delivery of the eucharistic prayer? How were the texts prayed or said? Was there any form of musical design accompanying them?

First, it is important to note that in this period it was customary in all churches of East and West to pray the text *aloud*. There are a number of reasons for assuming this. There are passages from sources of all sorts that take for granted that the faithful in the church could understand the text of the eucharistic prayers.[18] Moreover, we know that in general in the ancient world, prayers, certainly in public rituals, were prayed out loud.[19] To a certain extent, praying softly was even a suspect

[16] In this connection see particularly the critical remarks by J. Heinemann on the attempts to reconstruct "original" Jewish prayers, including the *birkat ha-mazon*; J. HEINEMANN: *Prayer in the Talmud* (Berlin/New York 1977) 37-76.

[17] For the question with regard to improvisation of eucharistic prayer in the early Church, see A. BOULEY: *From freedom to formula. The evolution of the eucharistic prayer from oral improvisation to written texts* (Washington 1981) (= The Catholic University of America Studies in Christian Antiquity 21).

[18] See for instance ROBERT: Le Canon chanté? 87-88.

[19] See P. VAN DER HORST: Silent prayer in Antiquity, in *Numen* 41 (1994) 1-25 (reprint in IDEM: *Hellenism-Judaism-Christianity. Essays on their interaction* (Leuven 1998²) 293-315; M. KLINGHARDT: Prayer formulas for public recitation: their use and function in ancient religion, in *Numen* 46 (1999) 1-52, p. 14-20.

practice. People feared, for instance, that magic or evil intentions were involved.[20] The custom of praying aloud, in any case during liturgical celebrations, must have worked its way through among Christians.

Next is the question of whether the eucharistic prayers were sung. Were particular techniques of singing in use?

Before we attempt to answer this question, we must first realise that terms such as "sing," "read," and "say" can create misunderstandings on our part. For people from the 20th and 21st century the contrast between "singing" and "saying" a text is greater than was the case in antiquity. That is because we live in a culture of reading, in which on radio and television, but often also in liturgy, texts are read aloud from a prepared script, into a microphone. This manner of reading aloud is of course far from what we term "singing." In antiquity that difference was less great, particularly when a larger audience was being addressed, without a prepared text and without microphone.

> As soon as the speaking crossed over into poetry, or when the speaking had an audience or ceremonial character of one sort of another, rhythmic and melodic elements that we today would term musical, or at least pre-musical, surfaced. One can then speak of music and song, even when terms that were associated with musical performance were not used.[21]

That means that we must formulate our question more precisely. For modern people, the manner in which the eucharistic prayer was delivered would have had something of "singing" about it, to the extent that public speaking in the strongly oral culture of antiquity would easily call up associations with "singing". The question, however, is whether in terms of musicality the delivery of the eucharistic prayers would have been distinguished from the techniques used by rhetoricians.[22]

[20] See VAN DER HORST: Silent prayer 300-302.

[21] J. GELINEAU: Music and singing in the liturgy, in C. JONES, G. WAINWRIGHT & E. YARNOLD: *The study of liturgy* (London 1979³) 440-454.

[22] It is interesting to note that the Roman rhetor Quintillianus complains about the (to his mind) objectionable practice many orators had of singing while speaking. In that connection he cites Cicero, who is supposed to have said that the orators of Lydia and Caria almost sung during the epilogues (QUINTILLIANUS, *Institutio oratoria* XI,3,58). See in this connection also J. JUNGMANN: Praefatio und stiller Kanon, in *Zeitschrift für katholische Theologie* 53 (1929) 66-94; 247-271 and W. THALHOFER & L. EISENHOFER: *Handbuch der katholischen Liturgik* I (Freiburg i. Br. 1912) 266.

I am of the opinion that the answer to this question must be negative. I arrive at that conclusion on the basis of the following argumentation:

(1) In the (admittedly scarce) sources from the first centuries that contain information on the eucharistic prayers, we encounter no allusions that would point to any form of song. Gelineau justly notes in the same source cited above that one must not draw too many conclusions from this. On the other hand, one cannot totally ignore this fact either. For instance, when the sources speak of "hymns," we do encounter terms which, according to prevailing understandings, must be translated as "singing."
(2) Also the fact that the eucharistic prayers afforded ample opportunities for improvisation would, to my mind, be a counsel for some restraint. Of course, improvisation and singing do not have to exclude one another. On the other hand, it is not easy to sing a text which is to a large degree improvised. At the very least, to do so would demand a specially trained celebrant. One may ask whether the frequently small Christian communities of the first centuries could often meet that condition.

One might enter the objection to this rather sceptical approach, that it treats somewhat abstractly the pre-Christian, and particularly Jewish milieu in which the early Christian liturgy arose. We know that forms of song existed, particularly in Jewish liturgy where Levites used to sing psalms in the Temple. We also know that from a very early date, with the reading of passages from the Bible and with the praying of prescribed prayers in the synagogue, use was made of simple melodies.[23] Would it not be obvious then that the first Christians continued these Jewish musical traditions, and that they, with the praying of the eucharistic prayer would have made use of the existing simple Jewish melodies?

[23] See, for instance, the following passages from the Babylonian Talmud: Megillah 3a en 32a; Berachoth 6a; Ta'anith 16a. See also: E. SCHLEIFER: Jewish liturgical music from the Bible to Hasidim, in L. HOFFMAN & J. WALTON: Liturgical music in Jewish and Christian experience (Notre Dame/London 1992) 13-58, p. 22-29; J. MCKINNON: On the question of psalmody in the ancient synagogue, in *Early Music History* 6 (1986) 159-191, p. 187 (reprint in IDEM: *The Temple, the Church Fathers and early Western chant)* (= Ashgate, Variorum Collected Studies Series 1998).

At first hearing, this manner of arguing sounds very convincing. Yet here too there is every reason to proceed very carefully. First, the relation between the early Christian worship service and the liturgical traditions of the Temple and synagogue is more complex than one might initially think. Christians were indeed greatly indebted to Jewish traditions for the development of their rituals, but on the other hand, they also very quickly moved off in directions of their own. As just one example, the Christian custom of singing psalms in the liturgy is probably not derived directly from the synagogue. It appears much more likely that in the centuries that followed the destruction of the Temple Jews and Christians each in their own way, more or less independently of one another, gave the psalms a place in their liturgical gatherings.[24] Further, it is important to keep in mind that the musical traditions of the synagogue developed only gradually in the centuries after the destruction of the Temple, and that in the time which saw the rise of Christianity these had not yet reached the stage that is presumed in the Talmud (fourth/fifth century).[25]

This does not mean that there was no singing in the Christian churches in the first centuries. There certainly was. Especially in some of the Eastern churches it appears hymns in any case very quickly became popular.[26] It is also highly conceivable that the Scripture lessons were declaimed or recited in a manner that was closely related to that of the synagogue and that comes close to what we would today call "singing", employing certain recitation tones or certain cadences. But everything points to these forms of song having been extremely elementary.

Further, with regard to the eucharistic prayer, there is still another factor which complicates the matter. To the extent that we can speak of song within Judaism in the period after the destruction of the Temple,

[24] McKinnon: On the question of psalmody; J. Smith: The ancient synagogue, the early Christian Church and singing, in *Music and letters* 65 (1984) 1-16; J. Maier: Zur Verwendung der Psalmen in der synagogalen Liturgie (Wochentag und Sabbat), in H. Becker & R. Kaczynski: *Liturgie und Dichtung. Ein interdisziplinäres Kompendium* I (St. Ottilien 1983) 55-90.

[25] For the development of the musical traditions of the synagogue, see Schleifer: Jewish liturgical music.

[26] This was particularly true for the Syrian speaking churches. Cf. S. Brock: Syriac and Greek hymnography: problems of origin, in E. Livingstone (ed.): *Studia Patristica* XVI (Berlin 1985) 77-81. Reprint in S. Brock: *Studies in Syriac Christianity* (Variorum Collected Studies Series 1992).

we are dealing primarily with the liturgy of the synagogue, not the prayers that were said elsewhere – for instance at home. But it is precisely to that category that prayers associated with meals belong. If it is indeed true that the eucharistic prayers of the Christians had their origins primarily in the Jewish mealtime prayers, then there is all the more reason to be sceptical of the supposition that these prayers were sung in one way or another.

Finally, the question arises if, and if so, to what degree the faithful participated in the eucharistic prayer by means of sung acclamations. It is my view that we can say nothing with certainty on this question. In any case it is clear that most of the acclamations we encounter in later prayers were not yet known in this period.[27] This is also true, specifically, for the Sanctus.[28] It certainly cannot be excluded that this text goes back to the Jewish kedushah, which was also used by Christians, for instance during a form of morning prayer or in Christian versions of the Amidah, also called the Eighteen Benedictions.[29] There is however nothing which indicates that in the first three centuries a sung Sanctus was anywhere a part of a eucharistic prayer. At other points in the eucharistic prayer there were responses from the faithful, particularly at the beginning, during the introductory dialogue and at the end, at the Amen. It is in itself conceivable that use was made of certain elementary forms of song for these, but the sources available to us say nothing on the matter.

[27] For information with regard to acclamations see M. SCHNEIDERS: Acclamations in the eucharistic prayer, in CASPERS & SCHNEIDERS: *Omnes circumadstantes* 78-100. See also A. GERHARDS: Akklamationen im Eucharistiegebet. Funktion und Gestalt im Liturgievergleich, in H.J. FEULNER, E. VELKOVSKA & R. TAFT: *Crossroad of cultures. Studies in liturgy and patristics in honor of Gabriele Winkler* (Rome 2000) 315-329.

[28] For the place of the Sanctus in early Christian liturgy, see R. TAFT: The interpolation of the Sanctus into Anaphora. When and where? A review of the dossier, in *Orientalia Christiana Periodica* 57 (1991) 281-308 and 58 (1992) 83-121. See also B. SPINKS: *The Sanctus in the eucharistic prayer* (Cambridge 1991) 57-121.

[29] In particular, a passage from the seventh book of the *Constitutiones Apostolorum* appears to indicate this (VII,35,3). See also G. ROUWHORST: Jewish liturgical traditions in early Syriac Christianity, in *Vigiliae Christianae* 51 (1997) 72-93, p. 81, 85-86.

4. After the conversion of Constantine

4.1. Developments in ritual and singing

The fourth century is rightly considered to be an important milestone in liturgical history. The fact that Christianity, in part as a consequence of the conversion of Constantine, became an acknowledged and privileged, and therefore also public religion, had major consequences for Christian worship. That is certainly true for the celebration of the Eucharist, and more in particular for the eucharistic prayer.

First, it is important to note that the setting of the liturgy in general, and of the celebration of the Eucharist in particular, changed radically.[30] The number of participants in eucharistic celebrations rose considerably, and the spaces which were used for them therefore had to be adapted. People now came together in church buildings, which generally had the form of basilicas. In part as a consequence of the rise in the number of participants, there was a growing inclination to ritualisation and dramatisation. As one example, one can think of the phenomenon of the procession, which arises and becomes popular precisely in this period, for instance with the entry of the bishop or with the offertory.

A phenomenon that certainly cannot remain unmentioned in this connection is the development in the field of liturgical song. This now begins to play an increasingly important role. Particularly sung psalms – responsive and antiphonal – begin to take on an increasingly important place in Christian worship. A passage from the *Confessiones* of Augustine in which the author worries about the pleasure that he experiences in the melodious manner of psalmody that is customary in Milan, and then tells how Athanasius of Alexandria demands of those who read a psalm that they use so little voice modulation that the reading is more like speaking than singing, is significant in this regard.[31] The English musicologist James McKinnon emphasizes that this passage does not stand alone, but is symptomatic of a much broader phenomenon, namely the rise of the "formal ecclesiastical music" that he considers to be a creation of the fourth century.[32]

[30] See for instance Wegman: *Riten en mythen* 106-111; 152-159.

[31] Aurelius Augustinus: *Confessiones* X,33.

[32] J. McKinnon: The fourth-century origin of the Gradual, in *Early Music History* 7 (1987) 91-106, here 105. (Reprint in Idem: *The Temple, the Church Fathers and Early Western Chant*). Cf. Idem: *The Advent project* (Berkeley, Los Angeles, London 2000) 35-59.

The alterations that the celebration of the Eucharist underwent in the fourth century were certainly not limited to the spatial setting and the dramatic and musical design. They decidedly also involved the texts, and not least the content and formulation of the eucharistic prayer.

(1) Certain elements which in the first three centuries generally were not regular components of the eucharistic prayers now do become so. That is the case for the institution narrative and the anamnesis which follows upon it, but for instance also for the Sanctus. This brings into being the classic structure to which the Second Vatican Council reached back for its liturgical design, and forms the model for the approved Roman eucharistic prayers (with several adaptations to the later Roman tradition).

(2) It is also important that the process by which the texts become fixed begins. For the first time, particular eucharistic prayers are set down in writing. From the monograph that Allan Bouley devoted to this subject,[33] it is clear that this process got under way in almost all churches during the fourth century. The writing down of eucharistic prayers led to there being less room for improvisation. The process by which the texts became fixed occurred more quickly in some regions than in others, however. The possibility for improvisation continued to exist considerably longer in Gaul and Spain than it did in Rome. In these regions people also continued to write portions of the eucharistic prayers themselves for longer.[34] In Rome, quite early the Roman Canon was instituted as the only normative eucharistic prayer.[35] This might be related to the typically Roman inclination to attach considerable importance to precise formulations. Already in pre-Christian Roman religion it was regarded as especially important that a prayer should be uttered precisely in the prescribed words.[36] Otherwise the prayer would not be efficacious, or could even have a dangerous result. Whatever the case, that express uniformity was not found in the less centralised Gaul. People continued to write their own texts there until the seventh

[33] BOULEY: *From freedom to formula.*

[34] BOULEY: *From freedom to formula* 169-196.

[35] BOULEY: *From freedom to formula* 200-215.

[36] H. VERSNEL: Römische Religion und religoser Umbruch, in M. VERMASEREN: *Die orientalischen Religionen im Römerreich* (Leiden 1981) 41-72, here 42; KLINGHARDT: Prayer formulas 14-20.

century, when the Roman Canon was gradually introduced.[37] For that matter, this was also true for some Eastern churches, particularly the West Syrian church, where even after the year 1000 new anaphoras were still being written.[38]

(3) The fact that the texts were set down in writing appears in general to have had the consequence that higher demands were placed on the literary and stylistic qualities of the texts. The Roman Canon is a good example of this. One finds in this text almost all the qualities of the literary style that is so characteristic of prayers from the Roman liturgy: attention to the rhythm of the sentences, for the alternation of stressed and unstressed syllables, for alliteration, parallelism and the use of synonyms succeeding one another, which has an intensifying, enhancing effect.[39]

4.2. Musical design

What, then, was the situation with the musical design of the eucharistic prayer, or, more broadly, with the manner of delivery?

In my view, little can be said with certainty on this issue. There are, however, no indications in the sources available that would point to there having been any essential changes immediately in this regard when compared with the centuries before Constantine. That means that the prayers were still said out loud, in the way that was customary in antiquity. In the course of this, use was made of certain rules and techniques from rhetoric, but the eucharistic prayer was not "sung" in the sense in which hymns and psalms were "sung".

In a somewhat later period, however, in any case after the sixth and seventh century, in a number of churches some shifts do appear to take place on this front.

(1) In a number of Syrian churches it becomes customary for the priest to softly pray the largest part of the anaphora, including what we would call the preface. It would appear that we first encounter this phenomenon in the writings of the East Syrian author Narsai (sixth

[37] BOULEY: *From freedom to formula* 181-196.

[38] BOUELEY: *From freedom to formula* 229-240.

[39] See especially C. MOHRMANN: Quelques observations sur l'évolution stylistique du Canon de la Messe romaine, in *Vigiliae Christianae* 4 (1950) 1-19 (reprint in IDEM: *Etudes sur le latin des chrétiens* III (Rome 1965) 227-244).

century).[40] In the same period the Emperor Justinian circulated a regulation that the anaphora must be prayed out loud,[41] which would indicate that this was not always being done. In place of praying the eucharistic prayer out loud, the custom had arisen of whispering it. The background of this phenomenon almost certainly lay in a certain experience of liturgy in which reverence and respect for the sacred played a large role.[42]

(2) In the Western liturgy, which in this case means the liturgy of the city of Rome, people appear to have taken a different course. In a number of sources stemming from the seventh and eighth centuries, we encounter information that would point to the eucharistic prayer there no longer being declaimed, and not prayed with a soft voice, but more "sung". This involves particularly the *Ordo Romanus* XV, which is part of what is called the *Capitulare ecclesiastici ordinis*.[43] There we read that after the introductory dialogue, the bishop who is celebrating the Eucharist lifts his voice and "says" the preface so that this can be heard by all. After the Sanctus there is the instruction that the bishop then begins "to sing with another voice and with another melody" (*canere dissimili voce et melodia*), so that this is only heard by those who are standing around the altar.[44] The interpretation of this text yields some problems, particularly because the various manuscripts provide several textual variants. It is my opinion, however, that Jozef Jungmann, in a 1929 article,[45] has convincingly shown that we must assume what happened was more or less as follows. The bishop sang the preface in a clearly audible manner. After the Sanctus his voice was only audible to those who stood

[40] Cf. E. BISHOP: Silent recitals in the Mass of the faithful, in R. CONNOLLY: *The liturgical homilies of Narsai translated into English with an introduction* (Cambridge 1909) (= Texts and Studies VIII) 121-126.

[41] See the so-called *Novella* 137 (edited by Schoell in Th. MOMMSEN: *Corpus iuris civilis* III (Berlin 1895) 695-699. For the various versions of this Novella, see BISHOP: Silent recitals 122, footnote 1.

[42] See E. BISHOP: Fear and awe attaching the eucharistic service, in CONNOLLY: *The liturgical homilies* 92-97.

[43] M. ANDRIEU: *Les ordines romani du haut moyen âge* III (Leuven 1974) 45-125. See also C. VOGEL: *Medieval Liturgy* (Washington 1986) 152-154; 168.

[44] OR XV,37-39.

[45] JUNGMANN: Praefatio 263-265. See also IDEM: *Missarum sollemnia* II, 135 and esp. footnote 42; J. FROGER: Les chants de la messe aux VIII et IX siècles, in *Revue grégorienne* (1948) 98-107, here 99-101; ROBERT, Le Canon chanté? 89.

directly in the vicinity of the altar and he used another melody, but nevertheless, he continued to "sing". The hypothesis that the whole canon was sung is borne out by another liturgical source from the same period, the *Ordo Romanus* XXVIII, in which we read that on Easter Saturday night the *Exsultet* is sung *quasi canonem*: like the Canon or as if it were the Canon.[46] Finally, it is interesting to place both passages alongside the oldest versions of the consecration of baptismal water. In the version from the *Sacramentarium Gelasianum Vetus* (mid-eighth century), at the start of the passage that begins with the words *haec nobis praecepta* – a passage which, like the *Te igitur*, has a supplicatory nature – we read the instruction *hic sensum mutabis*, that is, "change your tone here".[47] The *Sacramentarium Gregorianum* is even more specific, instructing *hic muta vocem quasi lectionem legens*, that is, "change your voice here, as when you read a reading".[48] In other words, from this point onwards, the celebrant changes to a reading voice, that is, the simple, unadorned recitation tone which is used for the Scripture readings. It is very tempting to combine these passages with each other, as Jungmann also does. Then we could propose that what happened was the following: the preface was sung to a particular melody which was more lyric in nature than the reading voice. After the Sanctus, when the intercessory portion began, the celebrant changed to a sober reading voice that was perhaps somewhat lower, and had fewer flourishes and less cadence. Furthermore, the singing at that point was also softer (and this practice could then have been the predecessor of the custom which arose in the eighth century of saying the portion after the *Te igitur* softly[49]).

[46] OR XXVIII,62. ANDRIEU (ed.): *Les ordines romani* III, 404.

[47] *Sacramentarium Gelasianum Vetus* 447 (L. MOHLBERG (ed.): *Liber sacramentorum romanae aeclesiae ordinis anni circuli* (Rome 1981³) 73. See also JUNGMANN: Praefatio 265-266. See for the meaning of the word 'sensus' in this connection J. JUNGMANN: Der Begriff 'sensus', in *Ephemerides liturgicae* 45 (1931) 124-127.

[48] *Sacramentarium Gregorianum Hadrianum* 374d. J. DESHUSSES (ed.): *Le sacramentaire grégorien. Ses principales formes d'après les plus anciens manuscrits* I (Fribourg 1979²) (= Spicilegium Friburgense 16) 187. This passage, however, is absent in several manuscripts, among them the old manuscript of Cambrai. In other equally old manuscripts, among them that from Marmoutier, though, it does indeed appear.

[49] For the rise of this practice, see JUNGMANN: Praefatio 253-255; IDEM: *Missarum sollemnia* 131.

It is important to view this data in the proper perspective. One cannot derive from this, as there may be an inclination to do so, that the whole early Church, certainly after the fourth century, would have sung the entire eucharistic prayer in this manner. In the first place, we are dealing with a Roman practice which existed in the seventh century, although it might be somewhat older. But from the other side, it also appears to be certain that in any case, for a long while, the whole Canon has been sung.

Why did people, in any case in Rome, move to singing the eucharistic prayer? In my view, the developments that liturgy, and more particularly the eucharistic prayer underwent in the fourth century and thereafter must have played an important role in this. To begin with, there is the changed liturgical setting, which to an important extent was defined by the presence of a large congregation, which the celebrant had to take into account in his manner of delivery. Further, it is highly probable that the establishment of a fixed text, which precisely in Rome was far advanced at a very early date (in contrast to, for instance, Gaul or Spain), played an important role. This created favourable circumstances for perfecting the text of the eucharistic prayer stylistically, but also for a musical setting for it, all the more because precisely such a strongly stylised, rhythmic text lends itself easily for a musical setting. For the rest, one can question whether in the long run a text that was being repeated over and over again can sustain simply being read. Does not a text become longer wearing when it is said to music, particularly if one can choose from different melodies? In fact, in the past it has only been in a number of Reformation traditions that the formulae for the Lord's Supper have been read aloud – but there one can also note that it is precisely these traditions where the celebration of the Lord's Supper was limited to several times a year.

One final observation. The Roman tradition emphasizes the singing of the celebrant. It is in the very first place the bishop or priest who sings. One can question if this does not further emphasize the "official" role of the minister. In compensation for the central role of the celebrating priest or bishop, it is true there was the Sanctus, which since the fourth century had been a regular part of the eucharistic prayer and that was sung by the faithful. But one has to acknowledge that the singing role of the faithful was limited to the Sanctus.

5. Developments after the eighth century

In a certain sense, in most Eastern and Western churches the development of the eucharistic prayer seems to have reached its final stages in the first half of the Middle Ages. In most liturgical traditions, after the eighth century there are no more new eucharistic prayers being written,[50] and the texts that are being used are now by and large fixed. That does not mean however that the manner of delivery simply remained as it was in the preceding centuries. At the very least this undergoes a change in one respect: both in the East and in the West it becomes customary that the celebrant prays the text, or at least parts of it, with a soft voice, so that it is not audible or understandable to the faithful in the nave of the church. In the West this was a simple matter: from the eighth century the preface was said or sung aloud, but the section after the *Te igitur* which then begins to be understood as the actual Canon is prayed softly.[51] In the Eastern churches, the matter is somewhat more complicated.[52] In several traditions, especially the Byzantine and Armenian, almost the whole of the eucharistic prayer is prayed with a soft voice. That does not, however, apply to what is termed the "ekphonesis", which closes the sections of the eucharistic prayer, and to the words of institution, and sometimes also, in the Armenian tradition, for a part of the epiclesis. In other traditions, especially the various Syrian rites and the Coptic, sections which are spoken aloud and passages that are prayed softly alternate with one another. Yet here again there is a difference between East and West. In almost all the Eastern rites the silence is filled with acclamations and hymns which are sung by the choir and/or the congregation (the "people"). Fundamentally, that does not happen in the West. Because of this, singing in fact played a larger role during the eucharistic prayer in the East than was, and is, the case in the West.

[50] Exceptions being the West Syrian and Ethiopian traditions.

[51] See JUNGMANN: Praefatio.

[52] For information regarding the various Eastern traditions, see J. HANSSENS: *Institutiones liturgicae de ritibus orientalibus* II, 1 (Rome 1930) 315-340; A. RAES: *Introductio in liturgiam orientalem* (Rome 1947²) 88-94; see in particular for the Byzantine tradition H. PAPROCKI: *Le mystère de l'Eucharistie. Génèse et interprétation de la liturgie eucharistique byzantine* (Paris 1993) 305-307.

On the other hand, the difference between East and West must not be exaggerated. From the second half of the Middle Ages it became customary, particularly in Masses employing multiple voices, to sing the Sanctus and Benedictus at the time when the priest was praying the Canon.

In the Eastern church, the practice as just described remains in place to this very day. In contrast, the Western churches have broken new paths. In the sixteenth century a drastic reorganisation of the liturgy for the Lord's Supper took place in the churches of the Reformation. Everywhere in those quarters this had the effect that the Roman Canon, but in fact also the traditional eucharistic prayer as it developed in the early Church, fell into disuse.[53] Only the words of institution, and in some churches – the Anglican and some Lutheran traditions[54] – the preface were left. To the extent that the Roman Canon was reflected in the Reformation Lord's Supper formulae, it is prayed in the vernacular and out loud. As far as I know, the only exception to this is that the preface, in those traditions where it is preserved, is sometimes sung.[55]

For centuries the Roman Catholic liturgy sticked to the practice existing in the Middle Ages, of the priest praying or singing the preface aloud, and reading the portion after the Sanctus in a soft voice. In the 1960s the Roman Catholic Church abandoned this practice. Since that time, a number of eucharistic prayers can be used, and these are prayed aloud, as a rule in the vernacular.

Once the Roman Catholic Church had opted for praying the whole eucharistic prayer aloud, the question naturally arose of the manner of delivering it. Should the text be declaimed, or rather sung, for instance, as once earlier in Rome, in a recitation tone?

As is known, Roman liturgical books offer the possibility of declaiming the eucharistic prayers, including the preface, without musical design. At the same time, in the second half of the 1960s and in the

[53] For the various classic Reformation Lord's Table formulae, see I. PAHL: *Coena Domini. Die Abendmahlsliturgie der Reformationskirchen im 16./17. Jahrhundert* (Fribourg 1983) (= Spicilegium Friburgense 29).

[54] For the complex question of the survival of the preface in the latter of these traditions, see H.B. MEYER: *Luther und die Messe* (Paderborn 1965) 172-190; W. REINDELL: Die Präfation, in *Leiturgia. Handbuch des evangelischen Gottesdienstes* II (Kassel 1955) 453-520, esp. 496-520.

[55] See REINDELL: Die Präfation 499-520.

early 1970s the possibilities for singing parts of the prayers were considerably expanded.[56] The first step toward this was taken in 1965 in the *Ritus servandus in concelebratione Missae et Ritus Communionis sub utraque specie*. This provides for the possibility that during a concelebration, the celebrating priests can sing a number of sections of the Roman Canon, namely the portion that begins with the words *Hanc igitur* through and including the Supplices section – in other words, the words of institution and the passages that precede and follow them.[57] The 1967 instruction *Tres abhinc annos* extended this possibility to non-concelebrated celebrations of the Eucharist.[58] In 1968 three new officially approved eucharistic prayers were published, and this publication provided melodies for the narrative of institution and the anamnesis.[59] As already mentioned at the beginning of this article, the Latin edition of the Roman Missal from 1970 likewise affords all these possibilities.[60] A final step was taken in the *Ordo Missae in cantu* of 1975, intended for the Congregation of Solesmes; in this edition can be found musical settings for all prefaces and the four eucharistic prayers, in their entirety.[61]

The Dutch translation of the Altar Missal offers significantly fewer possibilities for singing the eucharistic prayer. One there finds only melodies for prefaces and further for Eucharistic Prayer IIIB.[62] Moreover, in practice these possibilities are utilised only to a very limited degree. Even in sung eucharistic celebrations the song generally is limited to the Sanctus and several acclamations. Outside the official Roman books, the search for ways to give singing a larger place in the eucharistic prayer goes on in various places. In this connection the table prayers

[56] I here warmly acknowledge my debt of gratitude to A. Hollaardt, for the inventory of information with regard to this.

[57] *Ritus servandus* (Rome 1965) 37-39; 81-94.

[58] 'Tres abhinc annos'. Instructio altera ad <executionem Constitutionis de sacra Liturgia recte ordinandam>, nr. 10, in *Acta Apostolicae Sedis* 59 (1967) 442-448; R. Kaczynski: *Enchiridion documentorum instaurationis liturgicae* (Rome 1975) 296-302.

[59] *Preces eucharisticae et praefationes* (Vatican City 1968). According to the *Normae pro adhibendis precibus eucharisticis* (p. 11) the consecration epiclesis in the fourth eucharistic prayer in this publication can also be sung, but no melody is printed for this purpose. For the first eucharistic prayer reference is made to the *Ritus servandus*, in which the sung portion can already begin with the *Hanc igitur*.

[60] With the exception, however, of the possibility for singing the *Hanc igitur* from Eucharistic Prayer I and the consecration epiclesis of Eucharistic Prayer IV.

[61] *Ordo Missae in cantu* (Solesmes 1975) 234ff.

[62] *Altaarmissaal voor de Nederlandse Kerkprovincie* (Utrecht 1979) 1395-1402.

of the Dutch Huub Oosterhuis must be mentioned, a number of which can be sung in part or even in their entirety, and are also expressly written and composed with an eye to that.[63] With regard to other churches, it can be said that there too from time to time attempts are made to find suitable forms for singing eucharistic prayers – which, in the meantime, are being introduced (or reintroduced) in various churches of the Reformation. It is striking, in this connection, that the 1998 *Service Book* of the Dutch Samen-op-Weg churches includes a series of sung Table prayers.[64]

6. Conclusion

In his book on the musical design of the celebration of the Eucharist, Anton Vernooij proposes that the eucharistic prayer has always been characterised by singing, and also ought to be linked to singing.[65] I heartily assent to the second affirmation. I am in full agreement with Vernooij when he writes, "We are dealing with a prayer which is, to a great extent, thanksgiving. It expresses the amazement, thankfulness and praise of the congregation. If there is anything which should be sung, it is this." The eucharistic prayer not only seeks to communicate information, but is also an expression of feelings, and seeks to bring about an affective state among the faithful. Precisely where we are dealing with these illocutionary and perlocutive aspects of language, singing and music play an important role, as Judith Kubicki correctly emphasizes in her recent book on the Taizé music of Jacques Berthier.[66]

[63] See for instance *Liturgische Gezangen voor de viering van de Eucharistie (*Hilversum 1979) nr. 190, 202, 205 and 221 and the article that the late liturgist Hansjörg Auf der Maur (d. 1999) devoted to them: Hj. Auf der Maur: De tafelgebeden van Huub Oosterhuis, in H. Manders & H. Wegman (eds.): *Goed of niet goed? Het eucharistisch gebed in Nederland* part 2 (Hilversum 1978) 11-37.

[64] *Dienstboek. Een proeve. Schrift, Maaltijd, Gebed* (Zoetermeer 1998) 650-668. The SoW project includes three Dutch Protestant denominations moving toward church union.

[65] A. Vernooij: *De muzikale vormgeving van de Eucharistieviering* (Hilversum 1986) 45.

[66] J. Kubicki: *Liturgical music as ritual symbol* (Leuven 1999) (= Liturgia condenda 9), esp. 147-168.

At the same time I must confess that I have some doubts with regard to the first statement, and in particular with the assertion that the eucharistic prayer has always been characterised by singing. With regard to the first centuries, I would want to differentiate the statement somewhat. I myself would want to emphasize that the sung design of the eucharistic prayer has developed only gradually, chiefly after the fourth century, and then particularly in the Roman tradition.

I would want to add to this that the history of liturgy teaches that it does not in fact appear so self-evident that eucharistic prayers were actually sung. For the practice to really become established, a couple of conditions would have to be fulfilled:

(1) Sung eucharistic prayers presuppose a certain degree of ritualisation and a fixed text. A minimal requirement is that the text to a large extent will be committed to writing. It seems to me that the plea for a sung eucharistic prayer is not easily reconciled with the romantic yearning that looks back to the freedom and the possibilities for improvisation that the celebrant supposedly had (and apparently did have) in the eucharistic liturgy of the first centuries of Christianity.
(2) If a text is to be set to music, then it must be of such a level of quality that it lends itself to that purpose. It must thus possess certain literary and rhetorical characteristics and qualities. It is asserted that every text can be sung. But some texts are easier to sing than others. And some texts are extremely difficult to sing.

Next, if one moves to having the eucharistic prayer sung in whole or in part, the question arises of who will do the singing. The decisions made on this point will have major consequences. If, as was customary in the Roman tradition, it is chiefly the celebrant who sings, that serves to considerably magnify the distinction between the minister and the congregation. It can be asked in this connection, what happens when, at a concelebration, several priests sing the words of institution in the presence of a silent congregation! Going in the opposite direction, the role of the celebrant/priest is relativised if the congregation sings a considerable part of the eucharistic prayer, as is notably the case in some of the eucharistic prayers by Huub Oosterhuis. Of course, a good deal will depend here on the theological choice one makes. Does one emphasize that the priest acts *in persona Christi*, or is one's starting point that it is primarily the community which brings the offering of praise?

Further, a separate problem arises when the choice is made for reserving the text of the eucharistic prayer for the priest, but allowing the other believers to still participate by means of acclamations. The question then becomes how one integrates these acclamations in the eucharistic prayer. On that point the various traditions of the West and East appear to be far from satisfactory in all cases. One gets the impression that in the past the community all too often did not so much participate in the eucharistic prayer in their song, but rather filled the silence with elements of singing that displayed no clear substantive and thematic relation with the eucharistic prayer itself.

In this contribution, I have tried to show that one can distinguish various periods in the history of the liturgy which differ sharply from one another. Following from this, the question might arise which period is the most ideal. I would first answer that this is really a question which cannot be asked of historians. If I was asked such a question as an historian, I would be inclined to answer, none of them. All of the various practices that we have encountered have their drawbacks. That is true for the Roman tradition, which in the eyes of many too strongly emphasizes the role of the celebrant. On the other hand, the use of acclamations in the various Eastern traditions also calls up certain questions. There are further always liturgists who can not resist the inclination to look back with nostalgia to the first three centuries. It is my conclusion, however, that church music in this early phase does not have so much to offer us. Time is necessary for the development of a musical tradition.

We can learn much from the past. The past can be a source of inspiration. At the same time, models from the past also yield problems. We will therefore have to search for the solutions that are most suitable for the liturgy of today. Sometimes very good possibilities will be found by following well trodden paths. Sometimes whole new directions will have to be sought. When the one will have to happen, and when the other, will appear out of practice.

Joseph Gelineau

LA PRIERE EUCHARISTIQUE COMME ACTE DE LANGAGE DE L'ASSEMBLÉE

1. Vers les nouvelles prières eucharistiques

Quand j'ai commencé à m'intéresser à la liturgie, on ne parlait pas de la prière eucharistique, mais du Canon de la Messe. De son texte on ne pouvait avoir connaissance qu'en le lisant dans un livre. En ce temps-là, le Canon de la Messe était lu à voix basse par le prêtre, dans un livre. On parlait encore moins de 'repas eucharistique', puisque seul le prêtre communiait, et quand était autorisée la communion fréquente, elle se faisait en dehors du cadre de la Messe.

Ce sont les débuts du mouvement liturgique après la guerre de 1940 qui ont mis en valeur la prière eucharistique. Et le repas? Je me souviens avoir été dans une grande abbaye française où le Père Abbé a envoyé son théologien de service pour me critiquer: le renouveau liturgique commettait une grave erreur en disant que l'eucharistie était un repas, car l'eucharistie, c'est un sacrifice!

Lorsque nous étions à Rome après le Concile pour faire le nouveau missel de Paul VI, nous employions le mot de repas, à côté de 'sacrifice', avec prudence, parce que la Congrégation quand même veillait! Quant à l'ordo de la Messe, à vrai dire, nous n'avons fait que la moitié du travail, car nous étions concentrés sur le *texte* des nouvelles prières eucharistiques que nous allions proposer. Mais la prière eucharistique n'est pas qu'un texte écrit ou lu, c'est d'abord un *acte*. Il est vrai, on a bien mentionné qu'avant la prière eucharistique il y a une procession des offrandes avec un chant (lequel?); on a bien mentionnée qu'il y a un partage du pain, mais il se situe de telle manière après le *Pater noster*, suivi de l'embolisme, de la prière pour la paix et du baiser de la paix que la *fractio panis* n'a pas sa signification propre. Donc nous avions encore beaucoup de chemin à faire. Ce n'est qu'après que je suis parti comme curé dans de petites paroisses très pauvres que j'ai compris l'importance que l'eucharistie ne soit pas simplement une prière du célébrant dans lequel s'insère le *Sanctus* comme l'intervention du peuple, mais qu'elle est l'action de l'assemblée réunie qui célèbre le repas du Seigneur.

2. La prière eucharistique: acte d'un repas festif religieux

Il faut enraciner notre sens de l'eucharistie au moment du rite fondamental. Le rite fondamental est la célébration du repas du Seigneur. Quand nous baptisons, il est évident que le rite fondamental est l'eau, le bain d'eau. Quand nous célébrons la messe, nous avons souvent l'impression qu'il faut surtout dire des textes entrecoupés de quelque chose. Alors la révolution qui nous reste à faire est d'arriver à cette action globale d'une assemblée qui célèbre le repas du Seigneur dans la louange. Et cet enracinement du sens de l'eucharistie part du pain et du vin, qui sont les symboles de toute nourriture et de toute boisson qui peut donner la joie de vivre.

Tout part du simple fait d'apporter du pain dans un groupe qui va le manger: le pain qui vient de la terre et du travail des hommes. C'est déjà toute la création que représente d'une certaine manière le pain, la nourriture du corps qui donne la force et la vie. L'eucharistie implique tout le corps de celui qui va participer. Ce pain est objet de partage entre les convives, et les convives eux-mêmes se sentent liés par le fait de manger ensemble. Enfin tout cela regarde vers le haut, car vivre, vivre pleinement, ce n'est pas seulement manger un morceau de pain. Il s'agit d'un symbole de quelque chose de plus grand. Or, le symbole du vin dans la vie est encore beaucoup plus riche que le symbole du pain. C'est pourquoi dans le repas juif c'est sur la coupe que l'on disait la plus grande bénédiction de Dieu. Je ne veux pas évidemment contester cette richesse symbolique du vin. Alons regardons vers le bas: la vigne de France s'enracine très profond dans le sol pour tirer l'humidité; il faut s'en occuper toute l'année. Souvenez-vous des paraboles de Dieu et sa vigne qu'on trouve dans la Bible. Puis le vin est le signe de la vitalité, du sang qui bouillonne, de la joie, du chant et de l'ivresse. C'est-à-dire: l'au delà de notre condition actuelle. De l'autre côté, le vin est le signe de la fête, durant lesquelles le vin va avec la musique. Aussi, quand on fait des toasts et quand on choque les verres de vin, le vin est le signe des alliances, et enfin de l'amour et du mariage. Par-dessus tout, il y a la coupe des bénédictions (cf. 1 Cor. 10,16). Mais si une eucharistie commune, repas du Seigneur, ne draine pas toutes ces valeurs-là, il y a toujours une dimension d'humanité qui manque.

3. Un acte de parole entre deux actes rituels

La prière eucharistique est un acte de parole entre deux actes rituels qui en affectent le sens. La prière eucharistique n'est pas une prière quelconque mais une prière de la table, une prière du repas. Avant de manger on prépare la table. Avant le prière eucharistique on apporte le pain et le vin. Dans les liturgies orientales, le moment central est le chant du *Chérubicon*, l'hymne des chérubins, lorsque le prêtre apporte sur sa tête les saints dons sous un voile. Il traverse ainsi l'assemblée et il entre à travers l'iconostase dans le sanctuaire pendant que tout le chœur chante l'hymne des chérubins. C'est ainsi que toute l'assemblée est mise en route vers le repas du Seigneur quand on apporte le pain et le vin. En tant que curé j'ai pu sentir dans les assemblées l'importance de cette ouverture de l'eucharistie par une procession qui traverse l'église pendant que tout le monde chante. L'assemblée chante qu'elle accompagne le Christ qui va s'offrir à son Père. Lorsque, monté à l'autel après avoir reçu le pain et le vin, moi comme célébrant chantais 'Le Seigneur soit avec vous... Rendons grâce au Seigneur notre Dieu... Vraiment il est juste et bon de te glorifier Seigneur...' tout le monde était déjà dans l'action. C'est tout à fait le contraire de ce qui se passe maintenant là où tous les gens sont assis attendant que les oblats soient placés sur l'autel. Ces fidèles sont tout-à-coup réveillés par les paroles 'Prions ensemble' ou par le chant de dialogue de la Préface: 'Le Seigneur soit avec vous... Elevons notre cœur'. Situation impossible: le début de la préface 'Vraiment il est juste et bon...' n'a pas de support, ni de préparatifs!

Regardons maintenant comment se termine la prière eucharistique. Le prêtre chante 'Par lui, avec lui et en lui...' (la doxologie finale) et toute l'assemblée répond massivement 'Amen', suivi par un grand cassure dans le progrès. Normalement on devrait passer directement de la prière eucharistique au partage du pain. Anciennement il n'y avait ni *Pater Noster* ni baiser de paix ni autres prières avant la communion. Moi-même j'ai fait l'expérience plusieurs fois de passer immédiatement de la prière eucharistique au partage du pain qui se faisait d'abord en silence et sur lequel venait le chant du partage. Ici s'esquisse la communion. Ceci donne une densité extraordinaire au partage du pain.

La manière dont on s'avance pour partager le pain est très importante. C'est un moment qui demande un approche délicat. Quelle que soit la qualité des prières eucharistiques, elles seront inefficaces en partie si elles n'ont pas cet encadrement qui nous est donné dans la tradition des rites et dans la nature même du repas du Seigneur. De là provient la revalorisation de la procession des offrandes, qui pastoralement a beaucoup de poids, et du geste de partage qui est un *geste fondamental* de l'eucharistie.

4. La structure de la prière eucharistique: louange, action de grâce, demandes

Parmi les variantes assez nombreuses que nous connaissons dans l'histoire de la prière eucharistique, il y a quand même un fond commun qui est assez bien mis en valeur par des études récentes. Le dernier livre sur la prière eucharistique est d'Enrico Mazza.[1] Mazza, professeur de liturgie à l'université civile de Milan, a passé sa vie à étudier les 'paléo-anaphores', c'est-a-dire les bribes très anciennes de plusieurs siècles (Didachè, papyrus de Strasbourg, livre VIII des Constitutions Apostoliques). Il observe que, tout au début, on a dû partir des prières juives en faisant ce que Jésus a fait: il a pris le pain, il a pris le vin, il a dit une bénédiction, il a partagé le pain. Mais on ne sait pas un mot de ce que Jésus a dit en prononçant cette bénédiction. On sait seulement qu'il a dit une prière de louange. Alors l'Eglise a dû elle-même inventer sa prière et elle est allée chercher tout naturellement dans les sources juives: soit le *Yotser*, la prière du matin (qui est une prière de louange), soit – d'une manière plus spécifique – le *Birkat-ha-mazon* (la prière obligatoire à la fin de tout repas).

Cette dernière prière a trois parties. La première partie est une prière de louange. Il s'agit ici d'une louange adressée à Dieu pour la création, pour toutes les bonnes choses que Dieu donne à l'homme, en particulier pour la vie et pour tout ce qui la nourrit: le pain, le vin. La deuxième partie est l'action de grâce (*todat*), impliquant une attestation de ce que Dieu a fait dans l'histoire du salut en choisissant Abraham et un peuple auquel il a donné une alliance, ainsi que la terre. La troisième partie consiste aux demandes. On demande à Dieu que son regne vienne, que son peuple soit rassemblé à Jérusalem, que le temple soit reconstruit (aspect eschatologique). Or, cette progression: louange – action de grâce – demandes se trouve en fait structurer la totalité des

[1] E. Mazza: *L'Anafora eucaristica. Studi sulle origini* (Rome 1992) (= Ephemerides liturgicae, subsidia 62; Studi di liturgia, nova serie 24).

prières eucharistiques connues dans l'histoire, même si c'est d'une manière pas immédiatement reconnaissables.[2] Beaucoup d'anaphores anciennes sont des prières successives. C'est le cas du Canon romain dont la partie la plus ancienne remonte au troisième siècle, mais il a évolué jusqu'au sixième siècle. C'est une série de prières dont il y a trois principales qui sont à la base: louange, action de grâce et demandes. On peut dire la même chose des prières eucharistiques mozarabes.

5. Dynamique de la prière eucharistique

Tout cela crée une espèce de dynamique qui correspond à la structure même de la prière eucharistique telle qu'elle a été comprise par ceux qui, après Vatican II, devaient se rendre compte des archaïsmes du Canon romain. Pourtant le texte du Canon romain est extraordinaire: il y a là une théologie qui n'est pas si élaborée que celle de l'anaphore de Chrysostome et de Basile. Dans les nouvelles prières eucharistiques qui ont été proposées on retrouve cette dynamique. La prière eucharistique n'est pas linéaire. Elle n'est pas non plus répétitive ni cyclique comme par example une hymne. La prière eucharistique est dissymétrique, elle a une espèce de dynamique. Elle commence de façon très vive: le dialogue. Ce dialogue est très important puisqu'il a la fonction de *un* qui parle au nom de *tous*, fonction tout à fait normale dans toutes les cultures. Car lorsqu'il y a un repas de fête, c'est le personnage le plus important qui va porter un toast en l'honneur de ceux pour qui le repas est offert. C'est un acte du groupe à travers un. C'est la dialectique un-tous qui est nécessaire pour le fonctionnement de toute la société. Donc ce n'est pas une particularité de la prière eucharistique que le rôle prédominant soit confié à un. Mais dans la plupart des cultures, par exemple en Afrique, on ne peut pas prendre la parole devant un groupe sans avoir son assentiment. Là, le président de la célébration demande explicitement le consentement de l'assemblée avant qu'il commence la prière eucharistique.

La première partie de louange est la *préface* chantée, proclamée ou cantillée – ce sont trois niveaux de possibilités d'expression. Tout cela débouche dans le *Sanctus*:

[2] Cf. Mazza: *L'Anafora eucaristica.*

Sanctus, * Sanctus

J'ai une admiration sans limites pour cette mélodie, le plus ancien *Sanctus* de la tradition latine que nous connaissons et qui est pré-grégorien. On y a vraiment le mouvement même des chérubins qui se renvoient:

Sanctus, * Sanctus, Sanctus Dóminus Deus Sábaoth.

Vient ensuite la proclamation: 'Pleni sunt caeli et terra', suivie de l'acclamation 'Hosanna!' C'est une action formidable, à condition de lui donner sa dimension et son espace. On ne peut pas le faire sans sentir la spécificité du triple *Sanctus* dans cette mélodie: on va de proclamation à acclamation (deux pas); 'Benedictus qui venit... Hosanna in excelsis!' Dans ce *Sanctus* (bien connu puisqu'il est celui de la Messe des morts) il est à remarquer que le second 'Hosanna' ne finit pas comme le premier:

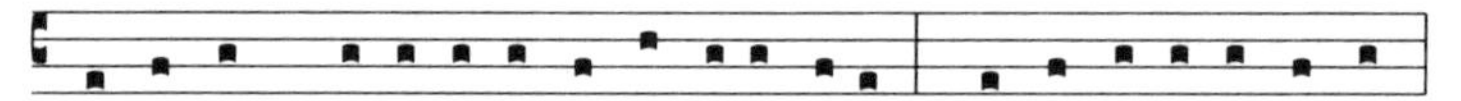
Ple-ni sunt cae-li et terra gló-ri-a tu-a. Hosánna in excélsis.

Ceci est la finale du mode de Si, mode répandu dans tout le bassin méditerranéen dans les premiers siècles. Et ensuite:

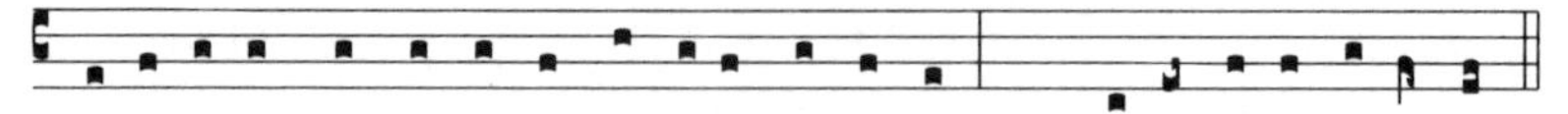
Benedictus qui ve-nit in nómine Dómi-ni. Hosánna in excélsis.

Ce phrase semble à finir en La mineur. En réalité, c'est une chute tonique. La tonique est dans:

Sanctus, Hosánna in excélsis.

Alors le président peut continuer:

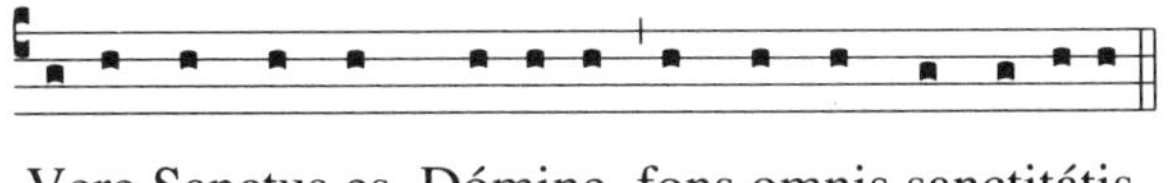

Vere Sanctus es, Dómine, fons omnis sanctitátis.

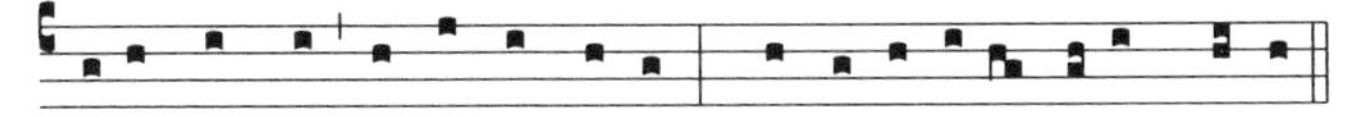

Pater noster, qui es in caelis : sanctificétur nomen tuum

C'est pourquoi je crois qu'il y a une loi fondamentale de la composition de musique du *Sanctus*. On ne doit pas finir ce chant dans un mode agité, parce qu'alors celui qui préside ne peut pas reprendre la parole. Mais quand on chante un *Sanctus* qui termine avec un accord piano long, le célébrant peut reprendre la phrase 'Tu es vraiment saint...' Toutes cettes particularités sont extrêmement importantes parce qu'elles semblent la condition même du passage d'un texte à la parole vivante.

A ce propos il y a un grand problème. Je m'en suis rendu compte un jour où l'on m'avait invité à une journée d'études à Paris de tous les responsables des Messes télévisées en Europe. On voulait mettre en commun tous les problèmes qui se posent. C'était une vaste quantité de problèmes, spécialement concernant la prière eucharistique. Or, chaque pays présentait une émission parmi celles qu'on avait faites. Après un enregistrement plutôt décevant d'une prière eucharistique parlée, commencée par un dialogue proféré en toute hâte et sans conviction perceptible avec des réponses routinières des fidèles, on nous montrait un document de grande valeur provenant de la Hongrie. Dans ce pays il n'y avait pas encore de Messes télévisées. Il s'agissait d'un film qui avait été pris dans une paroisse de montagne qui suit la liturgie byzantine en langue hongroise. Cet enregistrement commençait par l'offertoire. On y voyait sept hommes qui se sont avancés et arrangés devant l'iconostase. Il commencent le chant du *Chérubicon*. A ce moment le célébrant arrive et commence à faire l'encensement de l'église. Le diacre l'accompagne.

Puis, en partant de l'autel ils font la grande entrée, la procession des saints dons, en traversant l'assemblée. Toute la foule frémit et chante. Je n'ai pas compris un mot, mais j'étais saisi et bouleversé par cette action collective de louange et d'action de grâce. Après avoir vu ce document, le représentant allemand s'est levé et a dit: 'Comment est-il possible que nos fidèles comprennent que la prière eucharistique est une louange de toute l'assemblée adressée à Dieu le Père par le président, lorsque celui-ci lit simplement un texte dans un livre? A qui parle-t-il?' Les vrais problèmes sont d'abord là. Est-ce que le président de l'eucharistie peut rendre grâce au nom de tous en s'adressant à Dieu le Père? Je pense oui. C'est ce qu'il fait quand la participation de l'assemblée est spontanée, comme dans ce document hongrois.

6. Les modes du langage impliqués

Je voudrais insister sur ce que j'ai remarqué dans les modes du langage impliqués: ils rappellent les lois de la communication orale. En réfléchissant sur la prière eucharistique, j'ai pensé à la manière dont un conteur raconte. D'abord, il ne lit jamais dans un livre. Deuxièmement, c'est toujours la même histoire qu'il raconte. Troisièmement, il y a des moments sacrés. Or, nécessairement la prière eucharistique est une action de communicaton orale par la nature même de la louange adressée à Dieu par un seul au nom de tous. La louange est un *acte*.

Mais la liturgie en latin s'est transmise à nous uniquement par les livres et par la lecture, et nous avons perdu les lois de la communication orale. Au début du renouveau liturgique on a cru avoir un mode moderne de communication orale qu'était la télévision. Mais cela n'est pas le cas, car celui qui parle à la télévision ne s'adresse pas à un groupe, il s'adresse à chacun devant son poste. Donc il parle très vite sans sentir la réaction, il ne s'en rend pas compte. Nous savons que, dans la transmission que nous avons à faire, les mots comptent énormément ainsi que la manière de les dire. Or j'ai retrouvé dans la prière eucharistique toute la structure orale des histoires qu'ont racontées les mères de génération en génération à leurs enfants. C'est à dire qu'il y a là toute une tradition. Dans le *Mischna* il est dit que le rabbin qui doit dire les intentions de la prière ne doit jamais lire dans un livre. 'Celui qui lit dans un livre est un idolâtre'. Mais il doit réfléchir, pendant que tout le monde prie en silence, à la manière dont il va dire la prière. Il est sous-entendu que, chaque fois qu'on va prononcer la prière, il s'agit d'un cas unique. Et c'est ainsi qu'on peut comprendre le schéma qui se trouve dans la *Tradition Apostolique*, qui est devenu notre deuxième prière eucharistique. Il est dit en toutes lettres que ceci est un modèle, un exemple, un support, à partir duquel celui qui préside va dire la prière. Il ne s'agit ni de n'importe quoi, ni de n'importe comment; il faut respecter le caractère et l'ordre des choses, c'est-a-dire: des éléments constitutifs.

7. Conclusions

De tout cela on peut tirer quelques conclusions. Elles concernent les lois de la communication orale.

(1) En premier lieu, il ne faut pas toucher à la *succession des épisodes*. Il y a un ordre déterminé et invariant des épisodes succesifs dont se compose le récit entier: préface, *Sanctus*, *Post sanctus*, récit de l'institution, mention de notre union avec les saints. Toucher à cette succession est tromper les fidèles.

(2) En second lieu, je ne veux pas du tout affirmer qu'il y a un seul schéma possible de la prière eucharistique. Pastoralement j'ai pratiqué moi-même à une certaine époque toutes les espèces de prières nouvelles et j'ai pu me rendre compte qu'il y avait alors une difficulté pour la participation des fidèles et pour la communication. Ils étaient perdus! Il faut qu'il y ait des points de répère, des *mots-crochets* auxquels on se raccroche. Il est très important d'utiliser des formules typiques pour commencer chaque nouvel épisode. C'est exactement le principe de la lecture liturgique de la Bible dans le découpage des péricopes: il y a toujours des mots-chrochets qui font que cela commence bien et finit bien.

(3) Puis, il y a des moments variables: les *variantes circonstancielles*. Dans la prière eucharistique, si on l'adopte le schéma actuel de toutes les prières eucharistiques (sauf le Canon romain puisqu'il n'a pas cette structure), il est évident qu'il y a des moments qui permettent une certaine flexibilité pour amplifier ou abréger certains passages lorsque c'est utile. Dans toutes les prières eucharistiques nouvelles le texte du récit avant les propres paroles de l'institution

est différent. C'est fait délibérément et c'est extrêmement important, parce que, s'il n'y a jamais aucune variante, on n'écoute plus.

(4) D'autre part il y a des immuables. On n'y touche pas: certaines formules ont une valeur symbolique et sacrée comme les paroles de la consécration ('Ceci est mon corps... Ceci est mon sang'). Tout cela correspond avec toutes les lois de la communication orale telles que je les ai connues dans une civilisation orale et telles que je les ai redécouvertes en tant que président de l'assemblée.

(5) En cinquième et dernier lieu, il y a pour la *participation* de l'assemblée des moments codés et des signaux. L'histoire nous dit que, aux premiers temps, le prêtre qui présidait était le seul à parler entre le dialogue initial (qui semble avoir existé depuis les origines de la prière eucharistique) et l'*Amen* final. Dans l'évolution de cette prière, une des premières choses qui apparaissent est le *Sanctus*, qui, il est vrai, a été introduit fort tard à Rome (au cinquième siècle). Par ailleurs, dans la liturgie romaine la participation du peuple à la prière eucharistique n'a pas été très grande. Dans la liturgie de l'ancienne Gaule comme dans la liturgie celtique, les fidèles y participaient beaucoup mieux. Mais quand on a unifié tout l'Occident au moyen de la liturgie sous les Carolingiens, il ne restait entre le dialogue initial et l'*Amen* final chanté que le *Sanctus* auquel le peuple participait. Car tout se passait dans le sanctuaire par des clercs qui chantaient en latin et qui y faisaient leurs cérémonies. Mais dans d'autres liturgies les interventions du peuple ont augmenté considérablement. C'est ainsi qu'on voit paraître l'acclamation de l'anamnèse par le peuple et par les chantres (on ne fait pas toujours bien la distinction entre les chantres et le peuple). Certaines intercessions se sont introduites dans la prière eucharistique. Le comble se trouve dans la liturgie copte. Là il n'y a pas moins de dix-sept interventions de l'assemblée dans le seul récit de l'institution: 'Alors Jésus prit le pain', 'C'est vrai!', 'C'est la vérité!', 'Ceci est mon corps', 'Amen, amen!' etc. Dix-sept acclamations simplement pour le récit, cela serait un peu trop pour nous. Mais entre cela et rien, il y a des possibilités. En tant que curé je cherchais pendant dix ans la bonne manière de faire participer l'action qu'est la prière eucharistique. J'ai été tout à fait bouleversé, séduit lorsqu'en 1970 j'ai participé, avec les membres de 'Universa laus', à la prière eucharistique chantée par la chorale, le peuple et le célébrant dans la Dominicuskerk d'Amsterdam. C'est que j'avais cherché depuis longtemps comment la

prière eucharistique soit une prière de toutes personnes, l'action de tout le monde. Rentré à Paris je n'ai pas pu m'empêcher de rédiger une prière, texte et musique, et nous allions la chanter dans l'église de Saint-Ignace où nous avions une bonne chorale. C'était un grand moment. Je voulais continuer sur cette voie. Mais quand je suis arrivé comme curé dans une petite paroisse sans orgue, sans chorale, sans chantres, il me fallait un autre mode de participation de l'assemblée. Et aussi pour une raison fondamentale: c'est que dans la prière eucharistique chantée tout est écrit: texte et musique. On ne peut pas changer un mot ou autre, alors que moi je constatais que je ne puis être président de l'eucharistie, si je ne peux pas improviser à certains moments sans être toujours penché sur un texte inaltérable. J'ai donc cherché comment faire participer mon assemblée. J'ai trouvé qu'on peut avoir dans la prière eucharistique neuf endroits où l'assemblée intervient: au dialogue initial, au chant du *Sanctus*, après le *Post-sanctus*, après la première épiclèse, après la deuxième épiclèse, après les demandes et après la doxologie finale. Mais elle n'intervient pas toujours de manière spontanée, parce que j'ai repris le transit de l'ekphonèse grecque: vers la fin d'un texte parlé je commencait à cantiller. Ces ekphonèses à la fin des deux épiclèses sont suivies d'une supplication chantée par l'assemblée. Dans le récit de l'institution proféré sur un ton de 'citation' ou cantillée, il y a un double *Amen* (ou autre acclamation) des fidèles. Tout de suite après, la proclamation à haute voix de l'anamnèse invite à une acclamation de l'assemblée, tandis que la doxologie est suivie d'un grand *Amen* de tous. Le résultat est une prière eucharistique très courte et extrêmement alerte. Pendant cette prière personne n'a un livre dans la main: tout le monde chante par cœur et aussi le célébrant ne lit pas dans un livre. C'est ainsi qu'on arrive à une *action concertée*: la prière eucharistique comme acte de langage de l'assemblée.

Je pourrais faire la même chose avec un autre schéma, avec un autre texte de prière et avec d'autres réponses des fidèles. C'est une simple question de consensus du groupe qui doit se mettre d'accord sur la manière dont il va faire mémoire de ce que Jésus a fait. *Per omnia saecula saeculorum!*

Huub Oosterhuis

THE LANGUAGE OF LITURGY

The language in which we are born and raised and which we teach our children is like solid ground under our feet. Our native language is the foundation of the trust we have in one another and the "ground" on which we dare to move freely toward encounter with each other. We teach our children the words which go with things: chair, that is a chair; hello, chair beside the table; hello, tree – and there, that great warmth called "sun" and that beautiful coolness called "moon". Later we teach them the letters that go with the sounds; after speaking (and singing) we teach them to read and write.

We do not say or write "fish" if something is a snake, nor "bread" if it is a stone. We also teach our children what "good" and "bad" are; with the aid of these words we try to shape their conscience. Just as you can point to a rose and say "that is a rose" ('you are a rose'), we can point to what is evil and what is good, and we can even point to and name that which is love. Robbing people, stabbing them in the back, looking down on them because of the colour of their skin, war: these are bad, always. Kissing can be love, but it is never precisely the same as love; raising up a stranger who has been beaten down from the street where he lies, taking him into your home, washing his wounds, paying off his debts – it that love?

That familiar phrase from the first century of the Jesus Movement, "All things have their being through the word", can also be read as "all things are in their naming, exist by the grace of their name". Named by their name, they are present, recognisable, useful. But outside of language, outside the spotlight of naming, everything blurs and evaporates: what is that? a stone or bread? – that rubbish there – or is it a man? Without a name, or with the wrong name, we are lost, go missing, become confused by misapprehensions, arbitrariness, chaos. People who are nameless to us, or to whom we give the wrong name, are lost to us. If we do not use God's name, call on God – the original language of the Bible has only one word for both naming and calling –, if we name Him incorrectly, we lose touch with Him.

ℬ

Language is inexhaustibly rich, all words together, and all their possible combinations of meaning and sound. Each language is a galaxy, all the languages of the world together an expanding universe. Nothing is ineffable. Everything that exists in fact, in thought, in memory, in fantasy and dreams, can be said, described, denoted, conjectured, communicated understandably. Language is a spring, a treasury, a landscape. Memory and conscience. It has a sound, a cry for every pain. Every yearning has been sung at some time.

All the stirrings of the soul and perplexities of the mind, all the nuances of love and death have been written down at one time or another: floods of texts into which we can plunge, in which we can swim around, from which we can drink. We? Here we encounter a problem. Not every one of us, not all our children and their foreign classmates, are taught to take that plunge, or to listen, to taste, to identify. Not everyone in our midst has access to the treasure houses and the springs: much of what was once written with the intention of revealing people to themselves is now locked up, or made incomprehensible. Just as medicines are not accessible to everyone, so too words, the treasures of language, texts of revelation can be out of reach.

Language is an abundance of shades of meaning, nuances, images and metaphors. Poetry – which the poet Martinus Nijhoff (1894-1953) called "the glimmering language of the dawn breaking behind all evil" – is language in bloom. Poetry is a language of paradoxes: everything is nothing, here is far away, the I is the Other – my son was dead is alive again! "We are one", you percieve, counting four hands, two mouths. A word is a seed, a grain of wheat a man – words of bread, body of bread.

But, still, we do not communicate only by images and metaphors. Certainly: we also communicate in formulae, codes, definitions, statistics, abstractions and reductions – in paparazzi jargon, in free market jargon, in toe-curlingly corny language, in pub and sales counter commonplaces, in sex and death psychobabble – not to forget the primitive cries with which we assault heaven during our finest football matches. But in our liturgy, in preaching and prayer, when we sing, we serve each other with the language of the poets Nijhoff and Lucebert, which we recognise as being related to the language of the Biblical faith narrative – language about God.

𝔓

Is God ineffable, unutterable? There is a lot of religious secret language and jargon which creates that impression. God is a mystery – if he exists, that existence is certainly beyond all language. Words are inadequate to probe the deepest of all mysteries; you can not put it in words, so silence is better. The mystic poets of all world religions have taught us that. It seems to me purely felt and thought through: if God exists, he is beyond the reach of our language, and greater than our hearts.

In the Biblical narratives God is bigger than human language and the human heart. In the interpretation of these stories by Jewish and Christian mystic poets, it was – and is – emphasized that "God" is ineffable. We have learned from Judaism that when reading the Scriptures aloud, the Name of God must not be pronounced: there are four letters, JHWH, to be circuitously and approximately translated as "I will be who I am, I will be there", with the ring of "fear not". In place of the four letters which are not to be spoken, the synagogue says "Adonai". Yet the God of the Biblical narratives and songs is no "ineffable" God and no unutterable secret. The Bible stories say a lot about who he is and is not, how he is God, and how and where you find traces of his presence. That is loudly and openly declared, and all the social and political consequences of that are clearly articulated.

He is not spoken about in definitions, but in images and metaphors. Definitions exclude one another, images and metaphors embrace one another. The chemical definition of water cannot be both H_2O and H_30. In the Bible God is called light and a rock at the same time: he is as universal and important and immaterial as light, as enduring and solid as a rock – he stands there like a rock. In this same "poetic" manner the Bible stories speak of God as friend and father, about his hands and womb and countenance, that he is "in the heights", God in his heaven, in his hiddenness, but also that he descends to set at liberty. Images and metaphors, shades of meaning and nuances, glimmering language of dawn: that is the language of liturgy, proclamation and prayer, the language in which we sing. In the same way, the oldest witnesses, the epistles and gospels, speak of Jesus of Nazareth in images and metaphors.

𝔓

Neighbour. Stranger. Jew. Seed.
Tree beside a spring. Bridegroom. Way.

Dream of a man. Open door. Cornerstone.
Key. Lion of Judah. Lamb. Righteous one.

Shepherd. Pearl. Scion. Fish. Bread.
Word. Vine. Son of. God. Servant.

Streams of living water. Morning star. Pioneer.
One. Unutterable utterance.

Twenty-nine names. Who are we talking about? Jesus of Nazareth. Twenty-nine names were not enough to name all the memories of him: around what he evoked of the past, around the new future which showed forth in him.

As broad as the imagery of these twenty-nine names, just so broad is what the "first-born" experienced of him, and preserved in hundreds of brief testimonies, stories and sayings – the material from which the gospels were written, forty years or more after his death. In the Jewish style: hundreds of small stories, midrashim, flourish around the texts of the Jewish Bible – you have understood this, and you that, and you considered that? Good, we will preserve all these reflections and clever twists, all this pious wisdom, right around that great story, and carry them along in our daily, age-old encounter with the words we were once given. Without shunning anything that is outside of our acquaintance, broad and open. That is how Jesus' first followers dealt with him, after his death; he was prodigious, unutterably prodigious. Unutterable, but certainly spoken of, by approximation – and leave it at that.

But that is not where it was left. The sort of dogmatic formula that excludes all it is not familiar with appears to have won out over the broad, open image. In theological discussion and the preaching of the church, Jesus of Nazareth is primarily spoken of as Christ, the Christ, which means the Messiah – but in the word Messiah there are still echoes of many Jewish visions that are silenced in the word "Christ." "Christ" sounds like a mythic name for a mythic, supra-historical figure.

Christ, the means of expiation, the peace offering, "In Christ God was reconciling the world with Himself – Christ is the beginning, the first-born from the dead, he has made peace through the blood of his Cross." Compact, almost incantatory phrases in the letters of Paul, and those after him. Those who have been steeped in the churches somewhat longer – whether part of the Consultation on Church Unity or not – will know to what extreme formulations these words of Paul can lead: "[Christ] bore in body and soul the wrath of God against the sin of the whole human race, so that by his suffering, as the only expiatory sacrifice, he might redeem our body and soul from everlasting damnation...", says the Heidelberg Catechism, Lord's Day 15.

But in the course of the centuries Roman Catholicism too has retained little of the broad and open imagery and the many voices of the original witness, except for this reconciliation myth. Anyone making a pilgrimage through France – France, the oldest daughter of the Church, and the first "enlightened" nation in Europe –, who visits one magnificent cathedral after another, and has neither time enough nor an eye for the many and various sculptures, Jesus in more than twenty-nine forms and absolutely not a mythic hero – should they then end up in Vezelay on Sunday and attend the liturgy in the basilica there, what will they hear sung? "Lord, you have stretched out your arms on the cross, you have poured out your divine blood for a new covenant, you have turned away wrath from us, you have reconciled us with God, Alleluia!" And that is it. All the reformation movements in the world, and Roman Catholic Christendom after the Second Vatican Council, have only this Christ left, from all the original Jesus stories. In Vezelay and in Taizé, they sing the same unvarying, mythic, colourless formulas. "O Christ, Sovereign God and King in the Spirit, Alleluia!"

This has happened over the whole breadth of the Christian language field. In this way, the prevailing Catholic worship service has become an opaque mystery cult, no longer calibrated to the richly coloured images and metaphors of the Scriptural faith narratives. Christianity has become one of the great world religions, vague, inexact, calling upon the ineffable, unutterable. And the word "God" has become susceptible to interpretations of all sorts. The memory of Jesus of Nazareth, the celebration of the Eucharist, has become an opaque and indefinite ritual – however rigidly it is connected to one formula, the code of the "words of institution", without which it cannot be "legitimate".

It was in 1882, in his book *The Gay Science*, that Friedrich Nietzsche ascertained and announced the death of God, and compared this with drinking the sea dry and erasing the horizon: "And now we fall in all directions and wander through an infinite void." According to Nietzsche, the death of God means "that the highest values are devalued", that there is no longer any goal and no answer to the question of why. Henceforth all is in vain.

That God is dead and the earth uncoupled from the sun means that there is no longer any up or down, no direction and no point of reference, no shared starting point, and no authority that has any weight and offers security, that rules and reconciles. Implicit in Nietzsche's image is that there is no longer any parenthood, and particularly no "fatherhood". The God who is dead was the father god.

Nietzsche leaves no room for doubt about which God is dead: the Christian God. In his day the Christian God was first and foremost a vicious moralist, and in Nietzsche's milieu morality was chiefly bourgeois respectability. God was also an inscrutable ruler, exacting with his Ten Commandments, a severe Judge, a God of the next world who begrudged men this world. We are actually talking about many gods, although all Supreme Beings were then, as ever, experienced as one and the same: GOD, in three capital letters.

Now, we have learned, chiefly from our Jewish teachers (in a learning process that is for some of us in full swing, and for others just begun) – learned to distinguish between this Christian culture God and the God of the Bible, the God of Moses and the prophets. But in Nietzsche's day, the Bible testimony about God was still prisoner to Christian dogma, ecclesiastical codes and philosophic reflections.

In the Scriptural faith narrative, God is the liberator of slaves, a voice raised for the poor and oppressed, one that calls you to responsibility, asks "where is your brother, your sister". God is the one who proclaims this justice the criterion for a humane existence, and through the words of Amos and Isaiah and others pronounces a prophetic judgement against a world order that expels people, a world market in which the interests of poor and deprived do not count.

Nietzsche does not say a word about this God. When he predicts a future of "disintegration, havoc and ruin" he does not appear to have had even an inkling of the horrible misery that the Industrial Revolution of his century, the nineteenth century, had brought about: unprecedented forms of exploitation, uprooted masses, the "proletariat". For all the "wretched of the earth," God was, and is, dead, and the highest values were, and are, devalued. For them the horizon had been erased, and they were wandering through an infinite void.

We sometimes still live in the days of Nietzsche, in days of exploitation and rootless masses, and in days of a Babylonian confusion of tongues: what do we mean by that little word "God"? The Christian culture-God or the God of Moses and Jesus? What we desperately need is not an "interfaith" formula regarding God, but the Biblical name containing within itself the visions of a humane existence, a new world.

℣

Who or what is the "god" who is named "God" in our language? According to the Millennium Edition of the *Collins English Dictionary*, it is "the sole Supreme Being."

The majority of the sixty or seventy percent of the Dutch who say they believe in "something like a god", believe in a supreme being, something or someone, but beyond that can not clearly say what they believe. Or, for that matter, what "belief" is, how they do it, or how they came to it. Most are lost in their own phraseology, and contradict themselves: this stern Almighty is a great mystery, you can not entirely understand it, and thus you "believe" it.

In the book of Exodus I read and reread the passage in which Moses is summoned by name from out the burning bush. The summoning voice says that he is the God of Abraham, Isaac and Jacob, and that he has seen the suffering of the "children of Israel", that he has heard the cry of their oppression, and that he has come down to liberate them, to lead them out to a fine, broad land.

"I have seen, seen. And I have heard". How has he seen? Coldly and without compassion, with the derisive smile that we know from the faces of so many people?

"I have seen, seen" means: I have seen until I can take no more, until blind from tears I can look no more, and then I have come down from my heaven, from my throne, of my own accord. If you have ever sat on a throne, or even your own easy chair, in a high and comfortable position, you know that you must come down to be able to help someone. Thus it is written of God, "I have come down to rescue them from the hand of Egypt ('the House of Fear'), and lead them out to a fine, broad land."

In a world in which the word "god" still means "almighty power" and "supreme being," and in which millions are humiliatingly dependent on almighty powers, a god who comes down to liberate is completely unimaginable, a non-god. This one who comes down, this unimaginable one, is named "God" in the book of Exodus.

This God says, when he is asked for his name, "I will be that which I am. And how am I? I send you. That's what I am like – I send you to the oppressed children of Israel, because I have heard their groaning and seen their torment." The name of this God resounds throughout the whole Biblical story of liberation that begins here: that someone is sent to people in need. "That is my name until the end of days." To the end of time people will be sent to people in need – and let themselves be sent.

Give us proof that you are sent: lots of leaders have said that. Try it yourself: sent to set the captives free; perhaps just one captive, one disconsolate person who has a chance to get his breath again for a moment. You generally know that you are sent only when you come as one with a "calling". If you live with your ears open, you will hear cries, and know that they are meant for you.

℣

In her bestseller *A History of God*, Karen Armstrong is of the opinion that humanity must reforge its various motley images of god into one general god – no longer a Jewish God, a Christian, Islamic, Hindu, and Indian God, but "a general, preferably impersonal, but certainly merciful God."

I would point out to all who agree with her in this, who also rather like the idea, or see something in it – with an eye to "interfaith dialogue" – that I cannot conceive how you can do justice to the Biblical faith story (the most fundamental source for "Christian" thought about God) without emphasizing that it is not simply "god", but precisely this come down, sending-people-to-people-in-need non-god who makes himself known, "reveals" his name, in the context of the liberation narrative. When the exodus from the house of bondage has taken place, he gives the "ten liberating words" in which the vision of a just society is laid down. That is a "revolutionary political" vision.

In the Bible, "God" is a god of those ten words and of that vision. In a world in which murder and theft are accepted as political facts – in our world, in other words – the god of the Bible will want to be named after the victims, the murdered, the executed. In the story of Elijah, he is the god of those oppressed by the tyrant Ahab, even as in the gospel he is the god of the crucified. In the language of the psalms and prophets, to "deny his name" means to deny the victims. This is not an idea of my own; I have heard it and read it – to my dismay.

The word "God" is enmeshed in misunderstandings and bunkum. There is an unwitting language about God, a linguistic catchall in which everything is jumbled up together, from Biblical and "heathen" sources. And there are a lot of rumours about "god" in circulation. I suspect that many of those who come together in churches on Sunday unconsciously share in these, and become confused by these rumours, and are defenceless against them: they think that they are talking about the God of the Bible, but are really talking about an almighty supreme being. "Isn't God in fact omnipotent? But then he could have prevented Auschwitz. But he didn't. Thus he is an omnipotent sadist", an arbitrary god that deals out good fortune and adversity as he pleases. "Worse than the worst man," the writer Karel van het Reve termed this God.

It appears necessary to explicate the name of the Biblical God again and again, and to come to an understanding with the community of faithful that by "God" we mean that One who has heard the groaning of people and cannot bear their being demeaned, oppressed, forsaken or despised.

The God who demands compassion for the poor and deprived, the sick and the weak, who calls people to justice and love with the voice of the wretched of the earth, who wishes to be named for them – as the psalms and prophet's songs put it, "a god of the poor and dispossessed" – was in the days of Nietzsche kept alive by thousands of men and women who, in obscure groups, orders and congregations from the Salvation Army to the Sisters of Charity, knew themselves to be sent to care for the poor and dispossessed. He was kept alive by simple people, themselves entangled in cares and anxieties – not *Übermenschen*, but ordinary people, who did (and do) ordinary things, try to be as good as possible, for their children, their disturbed neighbour, the crazy person across the street, in the district, for the class. How far does that go? Farther than what is generally called "love". And that is how it will always be. Thus God will be alive when people are good – not "humanity", abstract, universal, but us, as good as possible.

The ritual of bread and wine, that gesture of breaking and sharing, however austere or ceremonious, surrounded by song – that is their life compressed into ritual. That is the gesture in which they make known their outlook, their messianic outlook, their following of the God of Moses and Jesus, who comes down to liberate, and sends people to people in need. They are in agreement that, if they say "God", they mean this One.

And on the basis of this "agreement about God" they can also agree on what they mean with the ritual of bread and wine:

those who set aside the work of their hands in this hour, take bread and eat, in doing so say:
that they desire a new world, where bread and freedom and justice are for all people. And choose to devote themselves to the fulfilment of that vision, with the force of a solemn promise.

℣

The celebration of the Eucharist is a vow you make to become a follower, and a promise that you will try to do what he has done and will what he willed. Breaking bread and drinking from the cup: a ritual in which you let it be known that you are in solidarity with all the hungry children of men, and are willing to share the fate of all who thirst after righteousness.

You do not need the literal "words of institution" to express that. They may be present, but they don't have to be. Moreover, in Catholic circles they still primarily call up memories of "transubstantiation". The far-reaching import of the Eucharist is safer in varying words. The ear quickly becomes accustomed to jargon, particularly to liturgical-theological jargon. The import of the ritual all too quickly becomes shrouded by that, and thus the original significance disappears from our consciousness, our memory, and our conscience.

In the spirit of the above reflections, I have written a Prayer for the celebration of the Eucharist. It should be sung. It follows here.

O Lord God
of whom we speak and sing
that You are merciful and ever faithful:

God of Abraham, God of Isaac,
God of Jacob, God of Moses and Elijah,
God of David, Ezra, Nehemiah.

You, the hope of the word
of the Scriptures of Israel
and of our hearts
that You hear the cry of mankind,
the cry for help, the bitter weeping
of people all over the world.

Who sees their suffering, knows their names,
who has come down to liberate,
who will come in your messiah.

Be still. All things are ready.

short silence

Supper of salvation:
that the messiah will be manifest
to us.
Bread of tears for the world
Wine to strengthen our hearts
foretaste of joy to come –
that the strength of hope
not forsake us.

all stand, if possible

Blessed are You for Jesus, who spoke for you,
your friend, like Moses; your servant Joshua
who led your people into a new land

who, light of light, born and not made,
came down for us and our sake,
to rescue us, as You did,

who was crucified,
suffered and was buried,
and rose again on the third day
who was and is and is to come

who speaks to us,
questions, encourages, comforts, exhorts,

who appears to us in the words of grace
"love one another".

And it happened
when he was there at table with them:
he took the bread and spoke the blessing;
he broke the bread and gave it to them.

Then their eyes were opened.

We remember his name
and what he has done,
for once becoming who he was,
your man;
for once coming where he is,
with You.

Being eternal, timeless here now,
foundation of all that is here and now,
coming eternally, something in all
someone more than all people

let your spirit come over us.

Lest we don't live at the cost of others
chasing all things, devouring all things

let your spirit come over us.

Before your Countenance
all who have gone before us on the path of life
forefathers, many generations,
from whom we have received the words,
learned to love.

Let your spirit come over us.
As the bread that we break
was sown in the earth
and was gathered together
and has become one,
so bring us together from far and near
in the kingdom of your peace.

Let your spirit come over us.

Here today, under the protection of your word,
as You of old have called your community together
everywhere in this world:

let your spirit come over us.

Before your Countenance
all who will come after us
children born from us, many generations
all who will inherit the world from us.

Let your spirit come over us.

Before your Countenance
our dead, name for name –
why must they die?
The dead of this century,
all those who have perished
in war after war.

short silence

Yours is the future,
light that is not extinguished,
love that lasts.

Amen, come what will.

May the sharing
of this bread and this cup
strengthen us in the hope
that a new world will come
where there is bread and love
enough for all.

bread broken and distributed
cups of wine go around

For Anton Vernooij

Louis van Tongeren

LITURGY AND THE MUSES
ON ARTISTIC CONTRIBUTIONS TO LITURGY

1. Liturgical renewal and the rediscovery of the community as the acting subject of liturgy

The century just closed was a tumultuous one in many areas. Two world wars racked the West – the Second World War also involving the East – costing millions of people their lives; atom bombs were used twice; the Iron Curtain was set up and dismantled; developing lands succeeded in shaking off the yoke of colonialism; industrial labour-management relations altered radically; space was discovered and explored, and man landed on the moon; scarcely through the consequences of the industrial revolution, the world now faces a new revolution in communications technology. Nor did the last century leave the church and religion untouched. Through growing ecumenical interest and the founding of the World Council of Churches, Christians of various denominations have been brought closer together and have broken through the barriers between them. In the Roman Catholic Church a reconsideration of all facets of Church life got under way, culminating in the Second Vatican Council.[1] After the stimulus for renewal the Liturgical Movement had already provided in the first half of the century, in a short space of time after Vatican II the liturgy was entirely renewed.[2] Because of the radical

[1] For a survey evaluating the effects of Vatican II across the whole field of ecclesiastical and social life, see the various contributions to the three-day international conference held at Louvain in 1995, thirty years after the close of Vatican II. Preparations are still ongoing for the publication of the introduction; see M. Lamberigts (ed.): *Vatican II and its heritage* (forthcoming). For the paper on liturgy, see L. van Tongeren: Liturgical renewal never ends, in *Ibidem*.

[2] Of the many publications on the background, rise, development and consequences of liturgical renewal, I will cite here only a first hand report regarding the whole renewal process by A. Bugnini: *Die Liturgiereform 1948-1975. Zeugnis und Testament* (Freiburg/Basel/Vienna 1988), and several surveys of the literature and of the experiences of those involved: T. Berger: Sacrosanctum Concilium in the 1980s. The literature between the two anniversaries (1983-1988), in *Studia liturgica* 19 (1989) 218-222;

consequences this change has had for the religious dimension in the lives of many people, from a Roman Catholic religious standpoint the twentieth century can be qualified as the century of the Liturgical Movement and liturgical renewal. Thus the Liturgical Movement would not be out of place on lists and surveys of events which affected people most radically, or of the most outstanding or influential figures of the twentieth century. There is, after all, no period to which one can point in which in so short a space of time so fundamental and far-reaching a change took place in the area of liturgy as during the past century.

A fundamental point of departure for this renewal process was the attention for the faithful or the people, presently often termed "the congregation". It is true one can distinguish various motives that helped to get this process of renewal under way and pushed it forward, but the place of the people played a prominent, and even dominate, role. For the rest, this does not mean that the people themselves were directly involved in the renewal. Nevertheless, in two respects the people were definitive for the orientation of the renewal: on the one hand, it was conceived from the congregation, and on the other focused on the congregation. The reconsideration of the place and position of the faithful led to a rediscovery of the congregation as the acting subject of the liturgy. People spoke of "community liturgy", a concept that Anton Vernooij often, and readily, employs.[3] The point of departure for this volume was formulated as "the conviction that the first and only party to perform the liturgy is the community itself". That liturgical ritual is

M. KLÖCKENER: 25 Jahre Liturgiekonstitution und Liturgiereform. Ein Bericht über Veranstaltungen und Publikationen zu diesem Anlaß, in H. BECKER, B. HILBERATH & U. WILLERS (eds.): *Gottesdienst, Kirche, Gesellschaft. Interdisziplinäre und ökumenische Standortbestimmungen nach 25 Jahren Liturgiereform* (St. Ottilien 1991) (= Pietas liturgica 5) 429-459; L. MADDEN (ed.): *The awakening Church. 25 Years of liturgical renewal* (Collegeville, MN 1992); J. WAGNER: *Mein Weg zur Liturgiereform 1936-1986. Erinnerungen* (Freiburg/Basel/Vienna 1993); A. NOCENT: *Le renouveau liturgique. Une relecture* (Paris 1993) (= Le point théologique 58); L. ZODROW: *Gemeinde lebt im Gottesdienst. Die nachkonziliare Liturgiereform in Frankreich und ihre Voraussetzungen* (Stuttgart 2000).

[3] See, for instance, A. VERNOOIJ: *De muzikale vormgeving van de eucharistieviering. Achtergronden en nieuwe ontwikkelingen van soorten en vormen in muziek ten dienste van de gemeenschapsliturgie* (Hilversum 1986), and IDEM: "Dan danst de kreupele als een hert..." (Jes. 35,6). Over de toekomst van de gemeenschapsliturgie, in L. VAN TONGEREN (ed.): *Toekomst, toen en nu. Beschouwingen over de ontwikkeling en de voortgang van de liturgievernieuwing* (Heeswijk-Dinther 1994) (= Liturgie in perspectief 2) 57-76.

performed collectively and communally is self-evident for the present generation, and almost sounds like a tautology to us. That is in itself amazing, as it means that within the space of one or two generations something that was increasingly absent from the Church for more than a thousand years has now been accepted as obvious. From the early Middle Ages until into this century, the faithful were more and more removed from the liturgy, and thus the cultus was increasingly reserved for the clergy.[4]

In order to fully be able to fulfil their role as acting subjects of the liturgy, it was believed that the people had to be made more conscious of the content and background of the liturgy, and that the liturgy itself had to be made more accessible. In order to achieve that, various initiatives were developed and implemented to encourage greater awareness and involvement. Among the places engaged in these initiatives was the centre of the Liturgical Movement, the abbey of Keizersberg, in Louvain, which celebrated its 100th anniversary in 1999.[5] There is neither the opportunity nor need to go further into that here. I will only raise one aspect of this liturgical design work that, to my mind, has continued to have its effects down to the present day, and has exercised a far-reaching influence on both the design and experience of liturgy, namely the instructional and catechetical aspects within it.

2. Catechetical and text-oriented approaches within liturgy

All sorts of activities and initiatives were begun in the context of liturgical renewal, usually focused on instruction and promoting understanding. Through courses and informative evenings people could fill in the gaps in their knowledge of liturgy. Bookcases full of brochures, books and journals have appeared since then, loose-leaf and hard bound, on

[4] See TH. KLAUSER: *A short history of the Western liturgy. An account and some reflections* (Oxford 1979²) 97-101; H. WEGMAN: De witte hostie, in R. STUIP & C. VELLEKOOP (eds.): *Licht en donker in de Middeleeuwen* (Utrecht 1989) (= Utrechtse bijdragen tot de mediëvistiek 9) 107-120; H. WEGMAN: "Genomen uit de mensen en aangesteld voor de mensen". De voorganger in de middeleeuwse liturgie, in IDEM: *Voor de lange duur. Bijdragen over liturgie en spiritualiteit* (Baarn 1999) 53-80.

[5] See E. VAN ERMEN et al.: *Loven boven, altijdt Godt loven. 1899-1999. 100 Jaar Abdij Keizersberg Leuven* (Leuven 1999).

the background and development of diverse aspects of liturgy; to this very day it appears that this stream of publications is not to be staunched.[6] Many individuals are actively involved in liturgy in the parishes, and we think it important that this group in any case should be kept up to date on the subject. We bombard them with information so that they know how the lectionarium is put together, what the criteria are for a good prayer, how the calendar is organised, and so forth. Or to put it in other terms: there is a lot of communication about liturgy at the meta-level. That calls up the question (and sometimes the complaint) about just how all of this is related to experiencing liturgy. But, to be brief: there is a lot of catechetic meta-liturgy directed toward understanding and knowledge.

The liturgy itself was also subject to a more catechetical or instructive approach. With the renewal of the liturgy, the rituals have been simplified and become more transparent, and the excesses have been eliminated. But, although the figure of the commentator has disappeared, it was still thought advisable that from time to time during the celebration the pastor or lector should explain why we do what we do. The catechetic slant of the renewed liturgy can also be seen in the fact that since Vatican II the Scripture plays a larger role, and its proclamation has been explicitly upgraded in value. Every ritual has been given its own Liturgy of the Word, with readings from Scripture. The frequent opening up of Scripture, as urged by the Constitution on the Liturgy,[7] is in itself a good thing, but at the same time the idea has arisen that the reading from Scripture also functions as a rational, substantive justification for the ritual. Ritual liturgical play can apparently no longer take place for itself, but must be provided with a sound foundation. This impression becomes still stronger when the proclamation or sermon shifts in the direction of exegesis and biblical interpretation, as the sermon sometimes necessarily must be designated when it is given by non-ordained worship leaders. The historical/critical reading of the Scripture has also acquired a monopoly position in liturgy, making didactic interpretation all the more dominant.

[6] See the extensive survey of publications which have appeared recently with background information and concrete and practical material, in K. JOOSSE: *Literatuuroverzicht liturgie* (Heeswijk 1999) (= Liturgische handreikingen 24).

[7] See the Constitution *Sacrosanctum Concilium* nos. 24, 35 and 51.

The substantive-instructive approach in the liturgy was in part a consequence of the composition of the commissions that were charged with carrying out liturgical renewal. The members of these commissions were historians and theologians, academics and bishops, who were strongly text-oriented. They had dug out old texts and were concerned about formulations and phraseology that would be theologically responsible in light of the tradition. The renewed liturgy was ordered right down to its details and set down in black and white in books. Liturgical renewal was essentially a renewal of the liturgical books. In part because of this, particularly for official ecclesiastical institutions, liturgy is primarily a textual affair, the content of which must be theologically and historically thought-out. As a consequence, this liturgy has been more focused on the letter than the spirit. The emphasis on the textual aspect contains within itself the danger that liturgy is approached with a yardstick. Texts are not only judged on their content, but also prescribed precisely. Thus a pastor is more likely to be called to render account, reprimanded or censured if an adapted or alternative text is used, than when the ritual design deviates somewhat. History shows that institutions which sit in judgement of such things have in the past certainly concerned themselves with the design of liturgy. Liturgical art has been condemned more than once, forbidden or even banned from the Church, not because of text, but because of creative expression.[8] At the moment, anyone who seeks space and wants to experiment on the basis of the official liturgy will find himself much freer if the texts are left untouched. Even the translations of official texts require much more precision than many generally realise.[9] Approved translations of prayers

[8] The criticism generally involved the quality, or the degree to which the depiction was thought to be shocking or offensive. See, for instance, the censors' archive of the Dutch St. Gregory Association (NSGV = Nederlandse Sint Gregorius Vereniging), which preserves their judgements on new liturgical music. Among the examples of visual art banned during the last century are the stations of the Cross by Aad de Haas and by Albert Servaes. The former has since been reinstated and can be admired in Wahlwiller, South Limburg; the latter, on which the ban has still not been rescinded, is found in Koningshoeven Abbey in Berkel-Enschot.

[9] The sort of scrupulous and oversensitive forms the debate on translation of liturgical texts could take on over the past decades sometimes becomes visible in most revealing ways in: K. JOOSSE: *Eucharistische gebeden in Nederland. Een documentaire studie over de ontwikkeling van de vertaalde Romeinse en 'eigen' Nederlandse eucharistische gebeden (1963-1979)* 2 vol. (Tilburg 1991) (= TFT-Studies 17).

have already become so sacrosanct that they may not be said in the local dialect. Such a ban on alterations does not apply to songs and all other components of the celebration, however;[10] apparently these elements are of less importance.

It is not in itself surprising that ecclesiastical institutions want to safeguard the theological purity of liturgical texts. It is, however, somewhat surprising that caution is exhibited only with regard to prayers. After all, possible dissenting beliefs are more likely to be spread through songs than prayers.[11] Many people know at least snippets of the liturgical song repertoire by heart, but could repeat a passage from a prayer only with great difficulty. Both Pelagius and Ambrose and Augustine were already aware of the power of the sung hymn to spread a body of ideas – deviant or orthodox – and get them to take root.[12]

Last but not least, the disparity in interest in the verbal aspect of the liturgy is aggravated by the introduction of the vernacular. People became conscious of what was being said, and this demanded clarification, explanation and elucidation. At the same time people discovered that descriptive and explanatory texts are inadequate. Liturgy demands a different expression, and needs another language, a poetic or "second" language, as it has been put since the end of the 1960s, using the words of Huub Oosterhuis (b. 1933).[13] It is striking that in liturgy primacy was bestowed on the verbal, while our culture became ever more dominated by visual forms of communication. The word has become word, according to a variant of the diagnosis of the renewed liturgy ("The word has become hoarse") by the Dutch literature critic Kees Fens

[10] According to a press release from the diocese of Roermond on the occasion of a dialect Mass on January 23, 2000, in Vaals, Limburg, celebrated by Bishop F. Wiertz; see *Brabants Dagblad* for January 24, 2000, page 13, and *Een twee een* 28 (2000) (no. 1) 11.

[11] Since the time this was written, an initiative on Rome's part to check up on song texts has been noted. The instruction *Liturgiam authenticam*, published on March 28, 2001, by the Congregation for divine worship and the discipline of the sacraments, not only sharpens the criteria for translation of Roman liturgical books, but also is directed toward the songs, of which it says, "they should remain relatively fixed so that confusion among the people may be avoided." To this end, within five years the Conferences of Bishops must see to "the publication of a directory or repertory of texts intended for liturgical singing" (no. 108).

[12] See for instance C. MÖNNICH: *Koningsvanen. Latijns-christelijke poëzie tussen Oudheid en Middeleeuwen 300-600* (Baarn 1990) (= Bronnen van de Europese cultuur 5) 15-17; 42-45.

[13] H. OOSTERHUIS: *In het voorbijgaan* (Utrecht 1968) 236-244; (completely revised edition Bilthoven 1975) 151-158.

(b. 1929) about thirty years ago.[14] In itself that diagnosis was not so bad for its time, although it is possible to have a difference of opinion regarding the label that you attach to it. Its tone was largely reactionary, stemming from a nostalgic retrospect on moments of high aesthetic quality from ecclesiastical history. It is also possible, however, to evaluate the accent on the verbal more positively, and to see it as an inevitable and necessary reaction to an individually defined devotional liturgical practice that was strongly focused on outward appearances. The liturgy which was in force until the renewals of Vatican II was, after all, heavily dominated by non-verbal elements. It was primarily addressed to the senses. Liturgy was an ensemble of stylised gestures, movements and actions by the various functionaries, of instrumental and vocal music, of the odour of incense that spread through the church, and of the special light that came through the stained glass windows. In this sensory stimulating whole, the word took a subordinate place, at least for the faithful, because they could not understand the language, a fact which additionally reinforced the mysterious character of the liturgy.

3. Altered relations between liturgy and the arts

The change and renewal which was carried through in all fields in the Church since the Second Vatican Council became visible above all in the liturgy. That was not so much because the innovations in the area of liturgy were the most radical, but because among the various facets of ecclesiastical life, people had the most intensive contact with liturgy. Furthermore, the nature of the liturgical renewal had great consequences for the experience of the liturgy. Liturgical-historical insights, pastoral engagement and new theological visions were perhaps at the root of the renewal, but these underlying motives played only a subordinate role in the experience, if people knew of them at all. Replacement of the concrete liturgical practice by rituals of a completely new design was more obvious, and one of the most noticeable aspects to be encountered in this was the particularly sharp reduction of elements appealing to the senses. A verbal and more rational approach came at the cost of the sensory, which, moreover, was of great importance for the

[14] K. Fens: Het woord is hees geworden, in *Kosmos en oecumene* 3 (1969) 214-217.

recognisability and familiarity of the ritual.[15] Many authorities dismissed the sensory dimensions as incidental, outward display, which did not belong to the essence of liturgy and only distracted from its content; liturgy must address people, and do so with the literal significance of the word. Furthermore, this "encumbrance", adjudged unnecessary, was too much reminiscent of a vision of the Church and of the experience of faith which had by now been disposed of. The earlier stately liturgy in a richly decorated church where there was lots to see, hear and smell, made way for a simple, sober, clearly ordered, understandable and unambiguous celebration in which everyone could take an active part. The separate elements and components were judged on the basis of their functionality, and on that basis were maintained or eliminated.[16]

Meanwhile, however, changes have been at hand for some time now. Over recent years one can perceive the tendency to emphasize the place of sensory elements in the liturgy more. There has been a search for visual design and new symbols and ways to revivify old customs in order to adapt them and give them a place anew.[17] The richly varied vocabulary of forms of the traditional liturgy has been resurrected and is being drawn upon again, and without lapsing into uncritically digging out old usages, restoring or copying dated designs from the past, the importance of sensory experience in liturgy has been rediscovered.

This revaluation of the sensory followed upon a period in which ecclesiastical art went through a deep crisis. Not only, as we have observed above, was there less attention paid to the contribution of the muses to ritual, and for artistic design in liturgy, but the renewed liturgy demanded different sorts of design in sound, word, gesture and plastic expression. Ecclesiastical art was expected to have a different function. Because of this, the traditional ecclesiastical art was uncoupled from the Church, and artists and the liturgy drifted apart from each other. In the

[15] See G. LUKKEN: *Liturgie en zintuiglijkheid. Over de betekenis van lichamelijkheid in de liturgie* (Hilversum 1990); IDEM: *Rituelen in overvloed. Een kritische bezinning op de plaats en de gestalte van het christelijke ritueel in onze cultuur* (Baarn 1999).

[16] For a critical approach to this development, see A. LORENZER: *Das Konzil der Buchhalter. Die Zerstörung der Sinnlichkeit. Eine Religionskritik* (Frankfurt a/M 1981).

[17] See the many examples collected in H. VRIJDAG: *Zonder beelden sprak Hij niet tot hen. Nieuwe symbolen en riten in de liturgie*. Vol. 1: *Het kerkelijk jaar* (Hilversum 1988); vol. 2: *Vieringen bij bijzondere gelegenheden* (Hilversum 1989); vol. 3: *Het zichtbare in de liturgie* (Baarn 1991).

last analysis, though, this distancing between art and liturgy can not be ascribed only to the renewal of liturgy. The general decline in Church involvement had its effect on the challenge to artists to translate their creativity into ecclesiastical or liturgical themes and objects. Artists, no less than so many others, became estranged from the Church. Another important cause through which art became separated from the Church lies in the more distant past and is connected with the developments that took place within art itself. For a long time the connection was close, because the Church was one of the most important clients for artists. For centuries painters, sculptors, architects, glass workers, silversmiths and musicians were in the service of the Church in all sorts of ways. This at the same time defined the objects that they produced, which were usually intended for liturgical use. This situation began to change when, after the Renaissance, art to an increasing degree freed itself from the Church and religion, to grow into an autonomous domain in the end, i.e. in the nineteenth century. From that time on artists felt themselves still accountable only to artistic laws and rules.[18] To the extent that religion yet played a role in these autonomous works of art, it was no longer obvious that it should be expressed in the traditional language of artistic forms from within the Church. Because of the nature of the commissions and the liturgical context in which it generally was expected to function, ecclesiastical art generally was a form of applied art. But to the extent that art became more autonomous, and thus considered itself to have less relation to the applied arts, it also became further removed from liturgy.[19]

Although the production of church-related art has decreased sharply, religious themes are not absent from contemporary art. The great difference is that the artist no longer makes use of the traditional language of artistic forms that visualises and corroborates existing dogmas, and is linked with classic devotions. The power of modern religious art lies rather in that it seeks to be the expression of a quest for the foundations and fundamental values of life, that it pregnantly visualises the search

[18] According to J. DE MUL: Echo's van een laatste God, in J. HOET (ed.): *Kunst na de dood van God* (Baarn 1997) 15. For the development in the relation between art and the Church, see the survey in P. SCHMIDT: Geloof en kunst. Een paradoxaal huwelijk, in *Collationes* 29 (1999) 227-253.

[19] Cf. A. VERNOOIJ: De taal van de ziel, in *Jaarboek voor liturgie-onderzoek* 14 (1998) 219-237, and SCHMIDT: Geloof en kunst 248.

for meaning in a world experienced as unjust. For this it often employs forms which go beyond existing conventions. Art does not serve to merely fascinate, but can also provoke. In this manner the artist's expression, arising out of his or her experience, stirs, sometimes shocks and challenges the audience (reader, listener, viewer, spectator), providing inspiration and help to people today who are themselves in search of a religious interpretation for life. Art breaks through the monotony of everyday perceptions, and the religious dimension in art involves us in reality and its fundamental dimensions in a changed way. Through the surprising perspectives that it affords us, art enables people to renew their communication with themselves, with their fellows, with the world and with God.[20]

4. Renewed attention for art and liturgy, and the exemplary function of liturgical music

The accentuation of the word and the altered relationship between art and the Church has not led to the estrangement of music from liturgy. I think that there are various reasons for this. First, we can give a nod toward the long tradition of church music. Even during the turbulent period of renewal and change in the liturgy, it was clear how much support the culture of ecclesiastical music had and how deeply rooted it was. There was an enormous production of new compositions in all sorts of styles, so that the repertoire not only became more pluriform, but was also considerably expanded. Various popular music groups, now become older or disbanded, had their origins in the liturgy of that time: begun as a combo for a youth choir, they exchanged liturgy for the concert stage. To this day, choirs represent by far the largest percentage of the many volunteers who are active in parishes. That music and liturgy did not lose sight of each other despite the emphasis on the rational and verbal can be further explained by the fact that language has always been an important vehicle for music. Music lends itself to entering into relationships with language, and that is true to an even greater degree for liturgical music, which from its very beginnings has been concerned

[20] According to K. ZISLER: Gegen den Verlust der Augen. Bilder und ihre Bedeutung für Mensch und Glaube, in *Theologische Quartalschrift* 175 (1995) 336.

with word/sound relationships.[21] A third element that I would list here involves the to a certain degree accidental circumstance, that in the Netherlands, the actual renewal of the liturgy was undertaken primarily on the basis of, and supplied with material by poet/musicians and musician/poets and language artists. How would Roman Catholic liturgy in the Netherlands look now if it was not a poet and composer who found each other 40 years ago, but a sculptor and painter? Where would we be today if Huub Oosterhuis had been a dramatist and Bernard Huijbers (b. 1922) a choreographer or architect?

Whatever the case, Polyhymnia was the only muse who was able to maintain a close connection with liturgy. Beyond that, the muses are badly represented in liturgy. Creativity, artistry and artistic design are on the wane. Creative imagination has made way for rationality and for cognitive insight and understanding. The question is, however, whether such an approach does full justice to ritual and liturgy. The deepening, religious or spiritual significance of ritual is not dependent on its intellectual merits or the mental capacities or intellectual powers of the participants. Ritual and religion appeal to the sensory and the imagination. Religious expression avails itself of metaphors, images and parables. Only in that way can that which is ineffable and elusive, that which refuses to allow itself to be restricted by definitions, be expressed, even falteringly and by approximation. Artistic creativity is essential for making this conception manifest for our senses.

In the recent past we have accepted chiefly the guidance of poets and composers. We have at our disposal high quality Biblical literature, religious poetry and liturgical music; we may count ourselves fortunate that we have composers who understand the art of catching in music what poets have been able to capture in metaphor. But to touch the person in his or her totality, more senses must be addressed. It is important that the muses work as a team to stimulate the senses in various ways.

Although the dialogue of the Church or of liturgy with the various muses has gone silent for a long time, various musicians have certainly kept this dialogue going, albeit not without problems, and they can perhaps be helpful in expanding the range of muses involved in the conversation anew; their experience could be welcome in bringing other arts into the liturgy. After all, in terms of content the interest is the

[21] See A. VERNOOIJ (ed.): *Toontaal. De verhouding tussen woord en toon in heden en verleden* (Kampen 2002) (= Meander 4) (in preparation).

same, as the liturgist Philip Harnoncourt (b. 1931) recently proposed. In nine propositions, he argued that as essential elements, song and music were indispensable for liturgy, and that is no less true for the other art forms, which therefore must also be integrated into liturgy. They are so essential to liturgy, because they lend their power to their symbolic effect, to their property of sharing significance directly and immediately, without further explanation and commentary.[22] In other countries too this need to encourage and intensify such dialogue between artists and the Church and liturgy is alive. The absence of contemporary imaginative expressions from the muses in liturgy is experienced as a grave deficiency there. Both the pope and various conferences of bishops have emphatically brought the importance of art to general attention.[23] In order to open up discussions on the visual arts and liturgy with artists, the German Liturgical Institute in Trier has mounted an exhibition of modern art.[24]

In the Netherlands too several initiatives can be noted which reflect the tendency in the direction of a revitalisation or renewal of interest in the relation between art and religion in general,[25] and between art and

[22] Ph. HARNONCOURT: Liturgie und Musik. Liturgiewissenschaft und Hymnologie. Kunst als Theologie, in *Theologische Quartalschrift* 177 (1997) 283-292.

[23] On April 4, 1999, at Easter, a *Letter to artists* from Pope John Paul II appeared. In a speech the chairman of the Austrian liturgical commission pleaded for a closer link between art and liturgy; see E. KAPELLARI: Eine erneuerte Ars celebrandi, in *Gottesdienst* 31 (1997) 1-3; IDEM: Der Glanz der Liturgie, in *idem* 12-13. The German conference of bishops published the brochure *Liturgie und Bild. Eine Orientierungshilfe* (Bonn 1996). In connection with this publication, see A. GERHARDS: Kunst und Kirchenraum, in *Gottesdienst* 31 (1997) 49-50; IDEM: Räume gestalten, in *ibidem* 57-59; IDEM: Liturgie und Bild. Vorstellung einer Orientierungshilfe der Arbeitsgruppe 'Kirchliche Architektur und Sakrale Kunst' (AKASK) der Liturgiekommission der Deutschen Bischofskonferenz, in *Liturgisches Jahrbuch* 47 (1997) 62-77.

[24] See *Gottesdienst* 31 (1997) 50.

[25] See the general initiatives of the foundation Prof. dr Gerard van der Leeuw-Stichting, and the new series of publications that they have been issuing since 1997 under the serial title *Onderbreking*. Cf. also D. VAN SPEYBROECK et al. (eds.): *Kunst en religie. Sporen van reële aanwezigheid* (Baarn 1991) (= Annalen van het Thijmgenootschap 79,1); E. VAN DE LOO, R. KURVERS & P. ELDERING (eds.): *Kunst van geloven* (Baarn 1996) (= Annalen van het Thijmgenootschap 84,1). Contemporary art and religion was the central theme of the exhibitions 'Jezus is boos' (Jesus is angry) and 'Eeuwig kwetsbaar' (Eternally vulnerable); see R. STEENSMA (ed.): *Jezus is boos. Het beeld van Christus in de hedendaagse kunst* (Zoetermeer 1995) (= Religie en kunst 2); G. LUTTIKHUIZEN & R. STEENSMA (eds.): *Eeuwig kwetsbaar. Hedendaagse kunst en religie* (Zoetermeer 1998) (= Religie en kunst 9).

liturgy in particular. In the field of architecture, one can note the competition for ideas for the construction of a building for Christian worship in the third millennium, sponsored by the diocese of Rotterdam in 1996, on the occasion of the 40th anniversary of its creation.[26] Young up-and-coming architects submitted diverse designs – as did also established names in the field. During a conference accompanying the competition, a plea was made for more intensive contact between architects and liturgists. In this context mention can also be made of the elliptical or polycentric concept of church building that has been frequently advocated in recent years.[27] Such a concept permits a less static use of the building and allows one to be more imaginative with the preexisting spatial layout. We now use the space primarily as an auditorium or a theatre. In doing so we deprive liturgy of its dynamism, which the polycentric concept could return.

There are many artists active in the realm of religious visual art. Contemporary examples can be admired at various museums. It is striking, however, that almost all of these works of art were created outside the ecclesiastical or liturgical context. It can be asked if the autonomous forms of religious art, which frequently – at least when first encountered – have a disorienting effect, can function well within liturgy. Has contemporary religious art not taken on another, primarily extra-ecclesiastical function? There are, however, examples in which contemporary art which does not correspond with traditional language of artistic forms has indeed received a place in liturgy (although generally in more experimental celebrations). In several cases, the primary focus there was on music,[28] but generally it involved religious visual art. These were primarily paintings, and to a lesser extent sculptures that were integrated

[26] See P. POST (ed.): *Een ander huis. Kerkarchitectuur na 2000* (Baarn 1997) (= Liturgie in perspectief 7).

[27] F. LÜTHI: Versammelt um Ambo und Altar. Ein Konzept für einen Kirchenbau, in *Gottesdienst* 29 (1995) (11) 81-83; K. RICHTER: Liturgisches Handeln und gottesdienstlicher Raum. Eine Verhältnisbestimmung aus katholischer Sicht heute, in R. BÜRGEL (ed.): *Raum und Ritual. Kirchenbau und Gottesdienst in theologischer und ästhetischer Sicht* (Göttingen 1995) 57-76; A. GERHARDS (ed.): *In der Mitte der Versammlung. Liturgische Feierräume* (Trier 1999); Th. STERNBERG: Eine Frage der Identität. Wie soll man heute liturgische Räume gestalten?, in *Herder Korrespondenz* 52 (2000) (8) 412-417; L. VAN TONGEREN: The re-ordering of church buildings reconsidered (forthcoming).

[28] See K. HOEK, W. OOSTERWAL & H. RUITER (eds.): *Nieuwe muziek in de liturgie* (Harlingen 1987).

into the liturgy from time to time.[29] A couple of times the direction of movement was in fact reversed, and art was not introduced into the liturgy, but liturgy travelled to the artwork in museums.[30] All of these are of course exceptions; in general it must be observed that contemporary artistic activities take a subordinate place in liturgy. To the extent that there is interest in art with an eye to liturgy and the Church, it is overwhelmingly with regard to the conservation and restoration of works already in the possession of the Church. Considerably more money is invested in that than in commissioning and acquiring new, contemporary works. It is therefore a cause for rejoicing that the diocese of Rotterdam has given commissions to three artists to submit designs for a contemporary depiction of the Emmaus story.[31]

I cannot find more than these few modest efforts to report. But perhaps they are signals that the tide is turning. If the experiences of musicians with liturgy can be productively employed in the dialogue with practitioners of the other arts, it will be beneficial for the contribution of the muses to liturgy. It is well known that the financial situation of most parishes is none too rosy. One may ask, however, if that must be an impediment to the acquisition of contemporary art works. After all, there is money found for the musical design of liturgy: collections of sheet music are purchased, and choir directors and organists receive financial remuneration, albeit modest. Why should a percentage of the budget not be reserved for investment in the other arts? And reserving one or two percent of the construction budgets for building new

[29] In the Netherlands, considerable research has been done in this field by the Groningen liturgist Regnerus Steensma. Various experiments are described and discussed in R. STEENSMA: *In de spiegel van het beeld. Kerk en moderne kunst* (Baarn 1987); IDEM: De receptie van de tentoonstelling 'Met de dood in de ogen' in de Grote Kerk te Leeuwarden, in *Jaarboek voor liturgie-onderzoek* 8 (1992) 169-204; IDEM: Hedendaagse beeldende kunst in protestantse kerkdiensten, in *ibidem* 9 (1993) 133-144; IDEM: "Jezus is boos" in de kerkdienst. Reacties op drie hedendaagse kunstwerken tijdens de eredienst, in *ibidem* 11 (1995) 223-258; IDEM: *Mysterie en vergezicht. Over het gebruik van hedendaagse beeldende kunst in de liturgie* (Baarn 1993); G. DINGEMANS, J. KRONENBURG & R. STEENSMA (eds.): *Kaïn of Abel... Kunst in de kerkdienst: twee vijandige broeders?* (Zoetermeer 1999) (= Religie en kunst 10).

[30] See M. BARNARD: Een kerkdienst in een museum, in M. BARNARD & P. POST (eds.): *Ritueel bestek. Antropologische kernwoorden van de liturgie* (Zoetermeer 2001) 56-62, and A. AUGUSTUS-KERSTEN: Liturgie in het hol van de leeuw, in *Eredienstvaardig* 16 (2000) 84-88.

[31] See *Een twee een* 27 (1999) 665.

churches or renovating existing ones in order to stimulate the dialogue with artists could also be considered. A relatively modest portion of the amount that must be gathered by fund-raising and soliciting contributions would then be applied structurally to having contemporary religious and liturgical art created. Such an initiative would stimulate the expression of faith and religion in the artistic vocabulary of the 21st century, and benefit the artistic calibre of the liturgy.

Ko Joosse

THE DESIGN OF SUNG EUCHARISTIC PRAYER HOW CAN THE EUCHARISTIC PRAYER BE EXPERIENCED AS A REAL *SACRIFICIUM LAUDIS*?

1. Introduction

Since the Second Vatican Council it has become clear that the development of the ideal community liturgy is a slow process, a process that is still going on today. At present there is considerable interest in the design of the eucharistic prayer. A particular locus of this interest is the effect that the process of the inculturation of the liturgy has on the celebration of this text of thanksgiving and praise. The central question in this paper is therefore, how the design of the eucharistic prayer, in particular in its sung form, can contribute to it being really experienced as a true act of thanksgiving and praise. After all, the eucharistic prayer is, according to the *General introduction of the Roman Missal*, "the center and summit of the entire celebration" (nr. 54). But is it actually experienced as such? On the contrary, rather than being a high point of the celebration, is it not frequently a low point?[2]

I will study here the possibilities and limitations of sung eucharistic prayer. Singing is indeed one of the ways to make it a high point in the experience of churchgoers. But singing is not the only manner. The delivery, whether spoken or sung, is intimately related to the use of space and body. The eucharistic prayer is more than merely a verbal text. For this reason I will also discuss the influence of the spatial design of the church building, the arrangements around the altar, and the posture and gestures of the celebrant and the congregation. In this we must be

[1] With thanks to my professional colleagues Richard Bot, Gerard Lukken, Anton Vernooij and Jos Wilderbeek, who were so kind as to go over earlier versions of this article critically and offer their comments.

[2] Cf. A. Gerhards: Höhepunkt auf dem Tiefpunkt? Überlegungen zur musikalischen Gestalt des eucharistischen Hochgebets, in E. Renhart & A. Schnider (eds.): *Sursum Corda, Variationen zu einem liturgischen Motiv* (Graz 1991) 167-177.

well aware that we are dealing with a fairly complicated matter, since in the design of the eucharistic prayer there are many aspects in play which must all cohere with one another. Hopefully this exploration will offer aid in the search for an adequate liturgical practice, in which the eucharistic prayer can really be experienced as a *sacrificium laudis*.

I will handle this subject in three steps. First I will deal briefly with the general role division for the eucharistic prayer. Next I will consider the non-verbal aspects that are involved with the design of this prayer. Last, there follows an exploration of the possibilities for singing the eucharistic prayer.

2. Role division

Who is the acting subject of the eucharistic prayer? It is not easy to give a simple answer to this question, as one can distinguish multiple subjects of the action. According to the *General introduction of the Roman Missal*, the eucharistic prayer is the presidential prayer par excellence. It is reserved to the priest. But at the same time it is also a prayer of the community. In fact, the priest prays "in the name of all the faithful, and of all present."[3] This drops us into the midst of the highly complex problem of the relation between the celebrant and the assembly, and we at the same time touch upon the no less complicated theological problem of ministry. However, within the scope of the present paper, we cannot go into these issues.[4]

In any case, we can determine that all eucharistic prayers are formulated in the "we"-form. The eucharistic prayer is the prayer of the congregation of believers, who turn to God the Father in praise, thanksgiving and intercession. However, the faithful do not do that on their own, nor under their own authority, but "through Him and with Him and in Him." Ultimately it is Christ himself who prays to his Father, and with whom we, the Church, as his Body, may faithfully and reverently join.

[3] *General introduction of the Roman Missal*, no. 10 (*Documents on the liturgy*, 1963, Conciliar Papal and Curial Texts (Collegeville 1982) abbreviated: DOL), 208 no. 1400. Cf. *Constitution on the liturgy 'Sacrosanctum Concilium'*, no. 33 (DOL 1 no. 33).

[4] See more detailed on this matter: G. Mattheeuws: Presiding at the Eucharist: Sacrament of the ecclesial Christ, in *Questions liturgiques* 81 (2000) 227-235; G. Lukken: De voorganger in het spanningsveld van de liturgie, in *Tijdschrift voor liturgie* 71 (1987) 259-278, and the literature cited there.

Christ is the primary acting subject of the eucharistic prayer, and because we belong to Him by virtue of our baptism and confirmation, we are included in his act.[5]

3. Active participation

How is the division of roles between the priest and the congregation manifested in the official Roman eucharistic prayers? The instructions on the matter are rather strict: the entire eucharistic prayer is reserved to the priest. According to the 1973 circular letter on the eucharistic prayers "only the sound of the prayer must be heard."[6] The active participation of the believers consists primarily in "listening in silent reverence" to this prayer. In addition, they "take part through the acclamations for which the rite makes provision."[7] There are four of these:

- the responses in the introductory dialogue;
- the hymn of the *Sanctus*;
- the acclamation after the institution narrative;
- the "Amen" at the end of the doxology.

It is precisely these instructions which are so strained with the experience many churchgoers have of the eucharistic prayer. People are expected just to listen passively for minutes on end. They actually take part actively for only a few moments. The problem is that, in our culture, listening silently is hardly experienced as being something 'active', as an *activity*.

During the post-Conciliar renewal of the liturgy, there were attempts made by policy-makers at various levels to increase the active participation of the congregation in the eucharistic prayer. After the publication of the three new eucharistic prayers (II, III and IV) in 1968, the need for greater participation was acknowledged in Rome. In the eucharistic

[5] Cf. Y. Congar: L'‘Ecclesia’ ou communauté chrétienne, sujet intégral de l'action liturgique, in Y.M.-J. Congar (ed.): *La liturgie après Vatican II: bilans, études, prospective* (Paris 1967) (= Unam Sanctam 66) 241-282.

[6] Congregation for divine worship, *Circular letter 'Eucharistiae participationem' to presidents of the conferences of bishops on the eucharistic prayers*, no. 8 (DOL 248 no. 1982).

[7] *General introduction of the Roman Missal*, no. 55 (conclusion) (DOL 208 no. 1445).

prayers for masses with children, which appeared in 1974, the number of acclamations was expanded. In the Netherlands in the 1970s there was an examination of the possibilities for permitting the congregation to join in saying certain parts of the eucharistic prayers, such as the epiclesis, the intercessions and the doxology. The objection was acknowledged that the congregation speaking along in these sections generally did little to increase the aesthetic experience. For the rest, the Dutch bishops put a stop to this practise with the appearance of the *Altaarmissaal* in 1979, because according to them it was not in harmony with the unique nature of the eucharistic prayer.[8]

The question how the congregation can participate in a prayer that has a presidential character, at least in its constituent components, remains thorny. How can the congregation participate in this prayer without eclipsing the unique role of the priest? Can the participation of the congregation be given shape in other ways apart from the acclamations? How can a really vital dialogue be created? And how can the prayer remain a unity, in which the inner movement that runs through it is not disrupted? Of course, all these questions are inextricably linked with visions on church, sacrament and ministry, but they are certainly questions which arise in the present discussion on the design of the eucharistic prayer, and are even more strongly felt when this prayer is sung.

4. Non-verbal aspects of design

Before I go into the possibilities for musical design of the eucharistic prayer, I wish to examine some other elements that are likewise important for the design of this prayer: space, posture and gestures. In addition to singing, these non-verbal elements in fact contribute in no small measure to the eucharistic prayer being really experienced as *eucharistia*, a true thanksgiving. Actually, this whole subject demands a separate, independent discussion. Proceeding from concrete liturgical practice, I will here, through a series of questions, bring several points of interest to the fore.

[8] See the brochure which appeared to accompany the Dutch Altar Missal: *Een eerste kennismaking met het altaarmissaal voor de Nederlandse kerkprovincie* (Utrecht 1979) (= Bisschoppelijke brieven 10) 16.

4.1. Spatial design

The delivery of the eucharistic prayer takes place in a space. This automatically raises questions regarding the significance of the spatial design of a church building for the experience of the eucharistic prayer. How is the space of the church laid out? Where does the altar stand in this space? Its position will, after all, determine the relation between the priest and the congregation. In this connection, three possibilities can be distinguished. The first is the situation in which the altar stands far from those present or is raised high above them. It then forms a "separate" space, an "opposition" to their space. In the semiotics of space, one speaks in this case of a polemic topical configuration. A second possibility is that, on the contrary, the position of the altar expresses equality. It then stands at a place to which everyone relates in the same way (contractual topical configuration). There is also a possible intermediate form. In that case the position of the altar on the one hand expresses equality in relation to those present, but on the other hand also opposition (polemical-contractual topical configuration).[9]

How is the congregation situated in relation to the altar? The spatial positioning of the altar undeniably influences the involvement of churchgoers in the eucharistic prayer as a prayer act. Would the experience of this prayer as a collective prayer of the congregation not be improved if the faithful could really be *circumstantes*? It does, after all, make a rather considerable difference for the experience if people find themselves in rows of pews one behind another or in a large circle around the altar, beside one another. For the rest, this gathering in a ring around the altar does demand a more flexible design for the church space than we generally have at the moment.

In this connection, the design of the altar itself is also important. Is the altar, with its decorations and symbolism, really the "center of the thanksgiving that the eucharist accomplishes"?[10] Is it a simple, modest table, or a massive and manifestly present sacrificial altar? How are the various attributes designed, and what is their place: the plate for the Hosts, the chalice, the altar cloth and the corporal, the candle sticks on

[9] This division is derived from G. LUKKEN & M. SEARLE: *Semiotics and church architecture. Applying the semiotics of A.J. Greimas and the Paris School to the analysis of church buildings* (Kampen 1993) (= Liturgia condenda 1) 48-52.

[10] *General introduction of the Roman Missal*, no. 259 (DOL 208 no. 1649).

or around the altar? In the last analysis, the expression of richly decorated gold objects is completely different from that of objects made of simple pottery. Even the clothing of the priest is not an indifferent matter. A beautifully designed chasuble or a decorative stole can contribute to the experience of festivity. These are all elements which have, perhaps not directly, but certainly indirectly an effect on the experience of the eucharistic prayer.

4.2. Posture

Further, the posture of both the priest and the congregation is of importance for the experience. In liturgy, physical posture is never without significance. How does the priest stand behind the altar? What spirit and what feelings does he express by his attitude? Does the *orante* posture that he assumes really express praise? How is this attitude assumed? For instance, at what angle do the arms stand to the body? Are the upper and lower arms extended or bent? How does he hold his hands? We are really dealing with very subtle elements here, which still can make a world of difference.

What posture is most suitable for the believers during the eucharistic prayer? The official instruction is that people stand "from the prayer over the gifts to the end of the Mass... They should kneel at the consecration unless prevented by the lack of space, the number of people present, or some other good reason."[11] In our regions it is the most prevalent practice that people stand during the introductory dialogue, the preface and the Sanctus. After that they kneel – in any case, during the words of institution – and then remain kneeling until the end of either the doxology or the Lord's prayer. The big question is whether changing physical posture during the eucharistic prayer is so felicitous. Does this not split the prayer apart? I must also note the unfortunate custom existing in many parishes of simply remaining seated during the entire eucharistic prayer, as is the custom for other prayers as well.

As for the unity of the eucharistic prayer, simply one liturgical posture, namely standing, is to be preferred. Standing is the best posture for expressing praise and thanksgiving, which are so characteristic of the

[11] *General introduction of the Roman Missal*, no. 21 (DOL 208 no. 1411).

eucharistic prayer.[12] Moreover, by maintaining one and the same attitude during the eucharistic prayer, the unity of the celebrating congregation is better expressed. If the priest is standing during the eucharistic prayer, why should the congregation need to assume a different posture? And why, really, should not all of the churchgoers be able to pray in the *orante* attitude? We can read from Christian iconography that in the ancient church the attitude of the congregation, particularly during the eucharistic prayer, was the same as that of the priest, namely with arms spread in the *orante* posture.[13] Precisely because the *orante* posture not only expresses praise and thanksgiving, but also evokes these emotions, it could contribute to the eucharistic prayer being experienced more intensely.

4.3. Other gestures

Gestures also are a part of the design of the eucharistic prayer. The question is here once again, do these underscore the internal movement of the eucharistic prayer, or, on the contrary, do they distract from it? Particularly during the institution narrative many gestures are being made, gestures that essentially "copy" what Jesus did during the Last Supper.[14] The rubrics of the Roman Missal underscore here entirely the view, traditional since the Middle Ages, that the consecration takes place *during* the words of institution. Other gestures too – such as sounding the church bell, ringing the altar bells, burning incense, kneeling by the acolythes before the altar, genuflection by the priest – make the words of institution stand out as *the* high point of the eucharistic prayer. The question is, however, whether these words should be so emphatically isolated from the rest of the anamnesis and the entire prayer. The abundance of gestures in this section detracts from, rather than strengthens the unity and dynamics of the eucharistic prayer. There would be a great deal to be gained if what presently is again being experienced to an increasing degree came to be expressed in the ritual design, namely that

[12] Cf. P. LEVESQUE, Eucharistic prayer posture: from standing to kneeling, in *Questions liturgiques* 74 (1993) 3-42, p. 40.

[13] LEVESQUE: Eucharistic prayer posture 38-39; D.C. SMOLARSKI, *Eucharistia, a study of the eucharistic prayer* (New York 1982) 112-113. Vgl. J. BAUMGARTNER: Der Vollzug des Hochgebets – eine unbewältigte Aufgabe (II), in *Heiliger Dienst* 38 (1984) 151-159, p. 153.

[14] Cf. H. WEGMAN: The rubrics of the institution-narrative in the Roman Missal 1970, in *Liturgia opera divina e umana. Studi sulla riforma liturgica offerti a S.E. Mons. Annibale Bugnini* (Roma 1982) (= Bibliotheca 'Ephemerides Liturgicae' Subsidia 26) 319-328, p. 326.

the consecration of the gifts does not take place at one moment, but during the whole eucharistic prayer.[15] And if one is to speak of a high point in the eucharistic prayer, is that not to be found rather in the praise of the Sanctus, in the anamnesis itself, and – at the end – in the doxology and the accompanying elevation of the gifts? For the sake of simplicity, at other moments in the prayer the gestures could be limited to the stretching out of the hands over the bread and wine during the epiclesis, and the indicatively pointing to these gifts during the institution narrative.[16]

5. Musical Design

Song and music are means of expression that far transcend the pure spoken word. According to the *Constitution on liturgy*, "a liturgical service takes on a nobler aspect when the rites are celebrated with singing."[17] In liturgy singing is thus not something incidental, but liturgical action in its true sense. This applies particularly to the eucharistic prayer, as "the centre and summit" of the eucharistic celebration. Based on its content, it should be sung rather than spoken. The act of singing in fact reinforces the performative character of this prayer.

5.1. Language and style

If then the eucharistic prayer demands a sung form, it must also be singable. A text which is already difficult to speak, because of sentences which flow clumsily or irregular rhythm, will be even more difficult to sing. It is true for all liturgical texts that they must "fit in the mouth." What, then, is the situation with the speakability or singability of eucharistic prayers in this regard?

[15] See A. Verheul: La valeur consécratoire de la prière eucharistique, in *Questions liturgiques* 62 (1981) 135-144.

[16] Cf. (though from an Anglican perspective) D. Gray: "Hands and Hocus-Pocus". The manual acts in the eucharistic prayer, in *Worship* 69 (1995) 306-313, p. 311-312.

[17] *Constitution on the liturgy 'Sacrosanctum concilium'*, no. 113 (DOL 1 no. 113).

To be sayable or singable, eucharistic prayers must fulfil certain linguistic conditions. One of the conditions, in any case, is that the language must be poetic. It is, after all, a matter of compression and imagery. They must sound good, flow well, radiate beauty. Further, the language must be symbolic, pointing above itself, calling up and making present that to which it refers. If it is good, the music will intensify this referential and evocative power. Finally, the ritual character of the eucharistic prayer requires that the language can be repeated without becoming shopworn or boring.[18]

Comparing the present prayers of the Missal to these criteria, there may be a good deal to be done in order to improve the language. The Roman prayers, for example, have a rather decisive character. A couple of examples can perhaps illustrate this point. In Eucharistic Prayer I for masses with children lines such as these appear (literally translated from the Dutch version):

- "Yes, God, You are really a good Father. You love us greatly."
- "You are a Father who always remembers his children and will not desert them. Therefore you have given Jesus to us."
- "All over the world there are people who thank you as we do," etc.

Is this really language which creates space and opens it up, that suggests and evokes, which is an impetus to true praise?

5.2. The spoken eucharistic prayer

Before going further into the possibilities for sung eucharistic prayer, I shall make a few remarks on the *spoken* eucharistic prayer. The most prevalent practice is in fact that the eucharistic prayer is spoken. Now, even a purely spoken prayer is in a certain sense musical: through the intonation, the tempo, the pauses, the accents. After all, it is precisely to speaking that the saying applies: *c'est le ton qui fait la musique*. A slight elevation of the voice, an emphatic accent, a phrase spoken slowly, or, on the contrary, quickly, a pause – these are all elements that can aid in the eucharistic prayer being experienced attentively and intensely. Concrete practice would benefit if celebrants were conscious of the fact that every form of speaking is unavoidably musical, that

[18] Regarding the criteria for liturgical language, see P. DE CLERCK: Le langage liturgique: sa nécessité et ses traits spécifiques, in *Questions liturgiques* 73 (1992) 15-35.

every word, that every sentence can gain or lose significance by the way it is delivered.

In this connection, it is worth noting what the 1973 Circular letter on eucharistic prayers from the Congregation for divine worship had to say about delivery:

> In reciting prayers, and particularly the eucharistic prayer, the priest is to avoid, on the one hand, a monotonous, uninflected style and, on the other, a style of speech and actions too personal and dramatic. As the one presiding over the rite, the priest should by his speech, singing, and actions help those taking part to form a true community that celebrates and lives out the memorial of the Lord.[19]

Moreover, the letter also draws attention to the importance of a sacred silence in order to ensure the full impact of the words and greater spiritual profit.[20]

Regarding the delivery, in practice there is a good deal to be improved. For instance, what priest really *prays* the eucharistic prayer? Why does it happen so often that the prayer is *read out* from the altar missal, during which the celebrant has his eyes constantly glued to the book, as if he is seeing the text for the first time and is afraid of straying? It is not unusual that this reading is done at high speed. It also often sounds as if it is being directed to those present rather than to the most holy and eternal God. The priest frankly looks out into the church. From the whole of the attitude and use of the voice, there is often little that would suggest that we are *praying* (praising, giving thanks, remembering, beseeching). In this regard, the Jewish liturgy could serve as a model. According to instructions from the Mishna, the *reading* of prayers during worship is simply forbidden. The celebrant will always actually speak the prayers from memory.[21] Is it too difficult for priests to also actually know at least some eucharistic prayers in their head – or, as English puts it so beautifully, *by heart*? It would benefit the practice of delivering the eucharistic prayer if celebrants took these two

[19] CONGREGATION FOR DIVINE WORSHIP, *Circular letter 'Eucharistiae participationem'*, no. 17 (DOL 249 no. 1991).

[20] CONGREGATION FOR DIVINE WORSHIP, *Circular letter 'Eucharistiae participationem'*, no. 18 (DOL 249 no. 1992).

[21] So J. GELINEAU: New models for the eucharistic prayer as praise of all the assembly, in *Studia Liturgica* 27 (1997) 79-87, p. 84. See also Gelineau's contribution in this book.

aspects into account: the outward aspect of a delivery as technically polished as possible, and the inward aspect of consciously, carefully praying, with devotion.

5.3. Possibilities for sung eucharistic prayer

How can the eucharistic prayer be sung? Between a completely spoken and a completely sung eucharistic prayer there are all sorts of intermediate points imaginable: spoken eucharistic prayers with sung acclamations, partially sung eucharistic prayers and completely sung eucharistic prayers.[22] Parenthetically, it is striking that in the *General introduction of the Roman Missal*, official rules for the singing of eucharistic prayers are entirely lacking. The only directive is found in the article on the importance of song – a general recommendation that

> in choosing the parts actually to be sung, preference should be given to those that are more significant and especially to those to be sung by the priest or ministers with the congregation responding or by the priest and people together."[23]

I will now successively examine a number of possibilities for singing the eucharistic prayer entirely or in part. I will be basing my examination on liturgical practice in the Netherlands since the 1960s.

5.3.1. Spoken eucharistic prayers with sung acclamations

The most prevalent practice is that the eucharistic prayer is spoken by the priest, whereas the Sanctus and the memorial acclamation are sung by the congregation. It is less often the practice to sing the introductory dialogue and the Amen. It will become clear that a spoken prayer with only sung acclamations is the minimal form for making the eucharistic prayer sound festive.

What is to be said on acclamations? An acclamation is really an exclamation, a shout. In liturgy acclamations are always expressions of the congregation endorsing a text which has immediately preceded them. They have an important function, because it is particularly in acclamations that the congregation is able to make known that it is subject of

[22] Cf. the typology of J. WILDERBEEK: De zang in het eucharistisch gebed, in *WINEK-Info* 3 (1979) 121-129.

[23] *General introduction of the Roman Missal*, nr. 19 (DOL 208, no. 1409).

the liturgy. A musical requirement is that acclamations can be learned without much effort, and must be easy to repeat.

The critical point with acclamations is how they link up with the rest of the prayer, both the sections preceding them, and those following them. This is particularly true for the Sanctus and the memorial acclamation. How often is it not the case that there is too long a pause before these acclamations begin, so that the tension built up during the prayer in fact crumbles like a house of cards? It is essential for a properly functioning acclamation that it really contributes to the continued movement of the eucharistic prayer, rather than serving to disrupt that progress.

With regard to the musical design of the Sanctus, it is important to keep in mind that this is a high point in the prayer. In fact, the Sanctus is the climax into which the preface issues. But does this acclamation also really sound like a high point, the collective song of praise of heaven and earth? And do we really hear its character as an outburst? More than the musical design, it is the way of singing that is important here. The most important point about an acclamation is not its musical design, but that the way it is done should be spontaneous, dynamic, emotive and ready. The best acclamations are heard at football games. And what happens with the link between the Sanctus and "Blessed he who comes"? According to the *General introduction of the Roman Missal*, the Sanctus is emphatically an acclamation of the entire congregation together with the priest.[24] If the Sanctus is not sung by the entire congregation, however, how does the alternation among the priest, choir and congregation take place? In practice, it appears to be possible to have the sentences "Heaven and earth are full..." and "Blessed he who comes..." led by priest or choir. In this case it depends on the manner of singing just described – also for those acting as cantors – whether the character of the Sanctus as an acclamation will come through.

A totally different set of difficulties exists for the Amen. This acclamation is so short that the moment has passed before you know it, unless it is developed more musically. This can be done by, for instance, having the Amen repeated, alternating between the choir and congregation, and by varying between one and more voices. Consideration could also be given to linking the Amen with another liturgical acclamation,

[24] *General introduction of the Roman Missal*, nr. 55b (DOL 208, no. 1445).

the Hallelujah. After all, this is also a song of pure praise. In either case, the question is how a musical setting is able to express the weight of this moment. Does the Amen really sound like a festive conclusion of the thanksgiving? Here too the key element will be how it is sung.

In this connection we must also make a remark regarding the Amen preceding the doxology. In the Netherlands quite a few parishes have the custom that those present participate in this text.[25] This is in a certain sense understandable. After all, in the doxology the praise comes once again to a high point. It is as if the congregation can no longer keep silent at this conclusion. They lift their voices and break forth in the praise of God's triune Name.

I have already referred above to the possibility for increasing participation on the part of the congregation in the eucharistic prayer by expanding the number of acclamations. This has been done in the eucharistic prayers for masses with children (Eucharistic Prayers IX-XI), among others. The question remains whether this "solution" actually meets the desire of the congregation for more participation in this prayer. The French liturgist Joseph Gelineau (b. 1911), who in recent years has diligently sought for possibilities to enliven the eucharistic prayer, has his doubts about this. He acknowledges that "if the acclamation is short, well formulated and easy to remember, it is the most simple form of active participation in the eucharistic prayer for the congregation." But he also lists a number of disadvantages. "Its simplicity is at the same time its weakness," he says. His experience is that "the compositions in which people constantly repeat these exclamations become boring and wearisome."[26] According to Gelineau, the constant repetition of a short acclamation is only popular in certain cultures, and he does not count Western culture among these. Moreover, extra added acclamations in a prayer threaten to put the brakes on the dynamics of the prayer rather than encourage it, "because each time they interrupt the actual text and obstruct its progress."[27] An acclamation is only a

[25] Although officially this practice is not permitted, in the Netherlands we have a number of different musical settings for this component. See, for instance, numbers 311-313 in the collection *Gezangen voor Liturgie*.

[26] J. GELINEAU: Het eucharistisch gebed als verrichting van de vierende gemeenschap (I), in *Gregoriusblad* 121 (1997) 205-210, p. 207. This article is a Dutch translation of a paper Gelineau held for the religious community of Bose (Italy) on 20 April 1994.

[27] GELINEAU: Het eucharistisch gebed 207.

good means of achieving active participation if it is used in a well thought-out way, and if it is, from the outset integrated into the totality of the text and action.[28] Whatever weight one gives to Gelineau's observations, in any case they do serve as a warning not to indiscriminately enliven the eucharistic prayer with acclamations.

5.3.2. Support by musical instruments or the human voice

Another way of making the spoken eucharistic prayer sound more festive is through accompanying certain passages with music. This practice is hardly known in the Netherlands, but elsewhere (Belgium, France and Germany) one regularly encounters it. The priest prays the prayer while the organ, as it were, accentuates the delivery by softly providing a simple musical background. This is done often during the institution narrative, sometimes beginning already at the epiclesis over the gifts, through the anamnetic prayer or the epiclesis over the community. It is the continuation of the practice, known for centuries now, of what is termed elevation music. Many *élévations* are known in the organ repertoire.

Strictly speaking, according to the *General introduction of the Roman Missal*, no instruments may sound during the presidential prayers, so that "everyone present listen with attention."[29] Yet the question remains whether the accompaniment really distracts attention. In any case, the instrumental support has the opposite intention, of fixing attention on that which is being said and done.[30] A disadvantage of this method is certainly that certain components of the eucharistic prayer will stand out more than others because of accompaniment. The same is true here as was already said regarding gestures during the words of institution. Such an accentuation will not always be helpful with regard to the movement and unity of the prayer.

A variation which should also be mentioned here is the use not of an instrument but of the human voice to support the spoken text. In the tradition there are songs following the consecration, called *cantiones*,

[28] GELINEAU: Het eucharistisch gebed 208.

[29] *General introduction of the Roman Missal*, no. 12 (DOL 208, no. 1402).

[30] Birgit Jeggle-Merz and Harald Schützeichel in fact argue for this practice in their chapter "Eucharistiefeier," in H. SCHÜTZEICHEL (ed.): *Die Messe: Ein kirchenmusikalisches Handbuch* (Düsseldorf 1991) 101.

both in unison and in harmony. Presently it is the practice, chiefly here and there in more southerly countries, for the choir to hum or sing in tenuto on a certain vowel (the a or o) during certain spoken parts of the eucharistic prayer (preface, institution narrative, epicleses, intercession prayer), thus preparing for the acclamations of the congregation. One achieves a movement toward a climax by doing this first in one voice and then in two, three or four voices.[31] It is a simple way of enlivening the delivery of the eucharistic prayer.

5.3.3. Partially sung eucharistic prayers

We saw that the most prevalent practice in the case of partially sung eucharistic prayer is to sing the introductory dialogue, the preface, the Sanctus and other acclamations. That was also what happened in part previously, before the renewal of liturgy of Vatican II. After the sung introductory dialogue, the priest followed with the singing of the preface in a recitative tone. Then followed the Sanctus and Benedictus by the choir, songs which sometimes lasted as long as the Roman canon itself, a prayer which was further recited in silence.

The Latin *editio typica* of the Roman Missal suggests that the eucharistic prayer can also be partially sung in other manners. For instance, in addition to melodies for the preface, the Missal also offers musical settings for the doxology, the institution narrative plus the anamnesis, and the offering prayer.[32] The Dutch *Altaarmissaal* offers melodies by the composer Floris van der Putt (1915-1990) for the opening dialogue and a number of important prefaces.[33] The preface tones (recitation formulas) are not difficult, and can therefore also be sung by a celebrant without long training. Yet many priests are evidently afraid to sing the preface, on the one hand perhaps because they do not dare, on the other hand because the awkward Dutch translation of the prefaces does not make them easy to sing.

The general objection to the partial singing of the eucharistic prayer is once again that the unity of the prayer is broken because the sung part receives unequal emphasis in comparison with the rest. The spoken

[31] We find an example of a similar manner of vocal accompaniment in MERZ & SCHÜTZEICHEL: Eucharistiefeier 102-104.

[32] *Missale Romanum*, editio typica altera (Typis Polyglottis Vaticanis 1975) 943-956.

[33] *Altaarmissaal voor de Nederlandse Kerkprovincie* (Utrecht 1979) 1373-1394.

parts will always sound less important than the sung elements. In any case, the singing of only the beginning (the dialogue through the Sanctus) is not an ideal practice. It awakens expectations which are not fulfilled, and contributes to a sense of anticlimax. Precisely as the praise is under way, it is broken off and the priest follows with the eucharistic prayer in spoken form, as if all that follows is only "second rate."

5.3.4. Entirely sung eucharistic prayers

Finally, the eucharistic prayer can be sung in its entirety. Which musical genres are most suitable for this? In the practice of sung eucharistic prayers, as it arose in the Netherlands in the 1960s and 1970s, three genres were most used: the recitative, the formula technique, and the song form.[34] It would be going too far to here report on how these functioned in the various eucharistic prayers.[35] The question now is what genre would appear the most suitable for the musical setting of the eucharistic prayers in the present *Altaarmissaal.*

[34] The DONEK data base (DOcumentatie NEderlandstalige Kerkmuziek), a data bank with all Dutch liturgical songs, employs a fixed classification into musical forms for the eucharistic prayer. Upon studying the scores and listening to audio tapes, however, it appears that this classification is inconsistent and inadequately thought-out. It ought to be revised in any following edition.

A more or less useful classification is suggested by Bernard HUIJBERS: Het juiste genre op het juiste moment, in *WINEK-info* 1 (1977) 121-124, p. 122. Huijbers successively distinguishes: 1. call, acclamation, dialogue; 2. recitation; 3. the "antiphon genre" or "motet genre"; 4. the song or hymn. Also based on this classification is A.J.M. BLIJLEVENS: Eucharistische gebeden en zang. Liturgische implicaties, in H. WEGMAN (red.): *Goed of niet goed? Het eucharistisch gebed in Nederland* part 2 (Hilversum 1978) 169-176, p. 171-172.

Ultimately, on the basis of the literature cited above, I have arrived at the three basic forms I have listed here: recitation, the formula technique and the song form. Cantillation could also be mentioned at this point. There is, however, no unanimity on this concept in the literature. It is used both in recitation and for the formula technique.

[35] An interesting investigation could be performed on the sung eucharistic prayers created in the Netherlands, analysing them on the basis of their musical genre and thereby tracing influence of the chosen form on the experience of churchgoers. In listing sung eucharistic prayers for the purpose of preparing this article, I got the impression, particularly in the case of settings by Bernard Huijbers, that they are very "ingenuously" composed. Possibly the study of these experimental eucharistic prayers and the experience gained with them at that time, could yield the necessary information for the choice of adequate musical forms for the official sung eucharistic prayer.

In any case, it is clear that the song form is unsuited for the eucharistic prayer. Without doubt, the song offers great possibilities for the active participation of the congregation in liturgy, but its closed form does not fit with the character of the eucharistic prayer. According to Gelineau, that is the greatest problem with the song in verses: it imposes a "static symmetry" into the eucharistic prayer. Moreover, with the song, even more than with the acclamation, a danger is lurking that the dynamics of the prayer will be broken.[36]

The other two genres, however, do appear suitable: the recitative and the formula technique. Recitation is the most simple manner of singing a text at an elevated tone. In recitation, the delivery depends entirely on the punctuation of the text. The text is sung at one tone (*recto tono*). Only at the point where a new sentence begins, where there is a comma, or where a sentence ends, an appointed modulation is made. There is no fixed formula which determines the melody. The formula technique is an extension of recitation. There the melody indeed has a fixed structure, a "formula" which regularly recurs, although it can be adapted to the text. The advantage of these musical genres is that they are able to express the movement of the text. According to Bernard Huijbers (b. 1922), the formula technique, despite all its disadvantages, is the only useful form for the sung eucharistic prayer, at least if one wants to let people sing along. Huijbers does acknowledge that the often capricious construction of eucharistic prayers calls for almost impossible demands on the formula technique.[37]

Recitation and the formula technique are certainly not entirely unproblematic as forms for the sung eucharistic prayer. For example, how can the peculiarities of the successive elements of this prayer be expressed? Is there a way to make audible the fact that certain elements have more the character of proclamation (preface, institution narrative, anamnesis) and other elements are more beseeching (epiclesis, intercessions)? Gelineau even has strong objections to the complete recitation of the eucharistic prayer. According to him, the musical form threatens to homogenise the inner dynamics of the prayer. Furthermore, he finds that reciting the entire prayer makes the role of the celebrant more prominent, producing precisely the opposite result to what is desired.

[36] GELINEAU: Het eucharistisch gebed 208.

[37] B. HUIJBERS: *Door podium en zaal tegelijk. Volkstaalliturgie en muzikale stijl. Zes en een half essay over muzikale functionaliteit* (Baarn 1994) 74-83, p. 83.

A complete recitation emphasizes and reinforces his role, and pushes aside that of the congregation.[38]

He himself therefore proposes the model of *ekphonesis*. He arrived at this after years of searching and experimentation, in both urban and rural parishes. *Ekphonesis* consists in the practice in which the celebrant, "delivering a prayer or part of it, at its end lifts his voice and 'cantillates' the final words, so that the choir or the congregation can immediately join in the answer."[39] This is comparable to what the priest previously did at the end of the Roman canon, where he began to sing the words *per omnia saecula saeculorum*, so that the community could answer with a sung Amen. *Ekphonesis* is also a practice which has always been maintained in Eastern liturgy: at the point of transition from speaking to singing the priest "elevates" the tone, so that the whole congregation can answer.[40] This is the best manner of guaranteeing the congregation's participation in the eucharistic prayer. The acclamations are introduced, or, better, called forth by the *ekphonesis*. In his experience, when delivered in this way the eucharistic prayer seems to retain its organic unity, in which the inner movement of the text is expressed in an adequate musical way.

6. Several questions and remarks in evaluation

I want to close this exploration of the possibilities for sung eucharistic prayer with some notes by way of recapitulation and evaluation:

(1) Rather than the prayer merely being spoken, its sung delivery can contribute to the eucharistic prayer being really experienced as a *sacrificium laudis*. The musical forms which are most obvious for this are the recitative and the formula technique.
(2) The participation of the congregation is guaranteed by the acclamations. The question is, however, whether the four acclamations of the present prayers in the Roman Missal are enough to do full justice to this participation. Expanding the number of acclamations would

[38] Gelineau: New models 82. Cf. Idem: Het eucharistisch gebed 209.

[39] J. Gelineau: Het eucharistisch gebed als verrichting van de vierende gemeenschap (II), in *Gregoriusblad* 121 (1998) 11-17, p. 14.

[40] J. Gelineau: *Libres propos sur les assemblées liturgiques* (Paris 1999) 76.

appear to be a solution to intensify participation. Yet this also has potential drawbacks, because there is a real danger of disrupting the dynamics of the prayer. For the rest, it would be advisable to further study what precisely the functions and effects are of the acclamations in the eucharistic prayer. To what degree do they contribute to the meaning of the whole eucharistic prayer? Do they perhaps work in the same way as in an antiphonal psalm, where the refrain always determines the direction in which the psalm must be understood?

(3) The *ekphonesis* model, suggested by Gelineau, is worth to be experimented with in the Netherlands. Both existing acclamations and, if necessary, newly composed ones, could form the basis for this. For the rest, Gelineau is correct in pointing out that people must respect the technique patterns of oral communication in this model. *Ekphonesis* also demands a less forced handling of the text in the eucharistic prayer. Some passages will always have a fixed and unchanging formulation, but others can be shortened or expanded as desired.[41] In any case, *ekphonesis* implies that the celebrant really knows the prayer by heart, and delivers it in the form of prayer.

(4) Many sung eucharistic prayers in the Dutch experimental practice of the 1960s and 1970s were for multiple voices. An important question to answer is what function multiple voices have in sung eucharistic prayer. What does this mean for the participation of the congregation? What effect does it have on the experience of the eucharistic prayer? And what, in this respect, is the role of the choir? How can a choir help the congregation in experiencing the eucharistic prayer as a particular act of praise and thanksgiving?

(5) Similar questions can be asked with regard to musical accompaniment. What is the function and meaning of musical instruments? Do they serve to support the song of the celebrant, choir and congregation? Or are they more illustrative? Do they provide an extra dimension? And do the qualities of various instruments play particular roles in the signification?[42]

(6) An important question regarding sung eucharistic prayers is that of practicability. A fully sung eucharistic prayer demands no small

[41] GELINEAU: Het eucharistisch gebed (II) 15.

[42] This is another point on which it would be interesting to further analyse the sung eucharistic prayers which were created in the Netherlands in the 1960s and 1970s.

musical competence from all involved – celebrant, choir, congregation and instrumentalists. If a sung prayer is to sound good, then all elements must in fact be perfectly ordered and attuned to one another. Where is that the case? How many parishes possess optimal possibilities in the area of church music? Or should we put the question precisely the other way around: is it possible with rather simple means to still evoke an experience of celebration and festivity?

(7) Following on from that, there is a general question: to what degree does the music still serve the purposes of liturgy in the sung eucharistic prayer? In the majority of Dutch sung eucharistic prayers, the music appears to be the dominant and defining element. If the music demands so much attention in the performance, is there still enough space for the content and movement of the prayer itself?

(8) It is good to sing the eucharistic prayer, to do full justice to it as a *sacrificium laudis*. It is important to realise that this can only take place in a liturgical practice in which the style of celebration and leadership is characterised by great devotion, care and concentration. For this all the Muses must be called into action, all forms of human expression: language, music, space, postures, movements. In all respects this is a matter of an "art" – the art of celebration, *ars celebrandi*. In this field we all – ministers and churchgoers alike – will have much to learn in the time to come.

Niek A. Schuman

SONG IN THE CELEBRATION OF THE REFORMED LORD'S SUPPER: RECENT DEVELOPMENTS

1. Introduction

What can the peculiar contribution of Reformed, or more especially Calvinist Christians be to this collection?[1] After all, unlike those who come out of the Lutheran or Anglican branches of the Reformation, *in liturgicis* they are undeniably late arrivals. The only thing that I have the courage to venture putting forward is the fact that precisely as a Calvinist liturgist I always still feel myself primarily *verbi divini minister*. And all things considered, can the *verbum divinum* not be expressed only in musical language and symbol?

On further reflection, it might also be useful to pause and examine that which is typical of and special to Reformed praxis with regard to the celebration of the Lord's Supper, precisely in the light of the main subject of this collection, sung eucharistic prayer. To that end I will first say something about the peculiarity of the "classic Reformed" Lord's Supper celebration, and then about more recent developments in the "ecumenical-Protestant" direction. In this, the emphasis will be on the sung components of both types of Lord's Supper celebrations. By means of this exploration, which will be chiefly of a liturgical-historical nature, I also wish to illuminate something of the spirituality of the Reformed Lord's Supper celebration. Subsequently I will make some observations regarding the place of the Psalms in the Lord's Supper liturgies, and by way of this arrive at a certain argument for a "Psalm mass" as a peculiar form, alongside other forms of sung eucharistic prayer.

[1] Prof. Schuman (b. 1936) is a member of the Reformed Churches in the Netherlands, a denomination which under the leadership of the politician Abraham Kuyper separated from the Dutch Reformed Church in 1886. There is presently a strong ongoing reunification movement (*Samen op Weg*).

2. THE CELEBRATION OF THE LORD'S SUPPER: DEVELOPMENT AND SPIRITUALITY

It is widely known that until well into the twentieth century the vast majority of local congregations and religious communities of Reformed descent[2] celebrated the Lord's Supper only a few times per year, and always under that name. It was therefore a very solemn service, often specially announced weeks before, with very specific preparations, in particular in the sermon and by means of home visits, during the week immediately preceding the celebration. At the Lord's Supper itself, there was first an extensive instruction and admonition given, being read from the order of service for the Supper. During the course of this, in the "Exhortation to Self-Examination," all who are impenitent were called upon to not partake of the Supper, lest they do so to their own judgement. But then for the contrite came the climax of the actual communion. This was celebrated at long tables, sometimes in several seatings because of the large number of participants. Each "seating" was preceded by and closed with organ music and congregational singing, generally in the form of rhymed psalms. I will return to this point. There were too many, indeed a true deluge of words spoken. Many people were drowned in them. Those who were able to keep their heads above water were confronted with heavy dogmatic explanations about what was indeed happening, and even more, was not happening there. The emphasis continued to be on the realisation of guilt and the call to penitence, albeit distinctly not without expectations. The Lord's Supper was indeed the foretaste of the Heavenly Banquet! All of this evoked that peculiar atmosphere of a sacred high point, notwithstanding all the words which were called up in response to these words. The songs and hymns, accompanied by God's own house instrument, the organ, made their contribution. Some sensitive souls were left with little benefit from all this. Others, also definitely not insensitive souls, got something rather curious out of it, largely associated with fear and trembling, as has been expressed in a number of Protestant poets.[3]

[2] The reformation of the church was definitively completed in the Netherlands around the year 1580.

[3] Cf. J.W. SCHULTE NORDHOLT: *Verzamelde gedichten* (Baarn 1989) 152-153.

2.1 The Liturgical Movement

Meanwhile, beginning in the 1920s the Liturgical Movement got under way, sparked by men such as J. Gerretsen (1867-1923) and G. van der Leeuw (1890-1950), at first primarily in the Dutch Reformed Church (NHK), but after World War II more and more also in the Reformed Churches in the Netherlands (GKN).[4] The Evangelical Lutheran Church in the Kingdom of the Netherlands (ELK)[5] already had a strong and venerable liturgical tradition. In 1955 they came out with a new hymn book and a revised order of worship with an *ordinarium* set to music. These songs to be used as part of every service are once again included in the ELK's liturgical collection of 1988,[6] along with a complete *ordinarium* set to music composed by Willem Vogel (b. 1920). Moreover, this supplement contains suggestions for what it calls a "Liedmis," a worship service in which rhymed hymns are to be used as parts of the *ordinarium*.[7]

The same year as the Lutheran's hymn book, 1955, the draft of the new NHK hymn book appeared. In it are included what are, in terms of the Lord's Supper celebration, classic, "didactic" orders, with longer or shorter expositions of the meaning of the sacrament. Then there is one with a somewhat more "celebratory" slant, albeit still strongly verbal in its focus. However, an order (Orde III) with a eucharistic prayer of catholic structure, with a sung dialogue, a Sanctus (without Benedictus) and Agnus Dei is really new. The inclusion of various optional prefaces that can be chosen is certainly also new, although these are rather tucked away, and printed in a literally "prosaic" fashion, not in units that can be spoken in one breath. In addition to musical settings of unrhymed "service music" there are suggestions for rhymed variants to be chosen from the NHK hymn book of 1938 – somewhat in the direction of the Lutheran's "Liedmis," in other words. The starting point is a

[4] M.A. VRIJLANDT: *Liturgiek* (Delft 1987, 1992²) 123-169; K.W. DE JONG: *Ordening van dienst. Achtergronden van en ontwikkelingen in de eredienst van de Gereformeerde Kerken in Nederland* (Baarn 1996) esp. 137-361.

[5] The voice of the Lutherans as a Reformation movement had been heard in the Netherlands beginning around 1560.

[6] *Liturgisch katern*, a supplement to the *Liedboek voor de Kerken*, the hymn book they shared with other Protestants (cf. footnote 9).

[7] H. JANSEN: Het 'gewone' van de liturgie; de lutherse traditie, in *Eredienstvaardig* 15 (1999) 189-191.

communion celebrated at and around a table in one seating. After the communion appear rhymed couplets of psalms such as Psalm 103 and 118. All in all, it was a momentous step forward in the direction of an ecumenical/Protestant, or, if one prefers, catholic/Protestant Lord's eucharistic liturgy.

These were the same 1950s and '60s in which a Gideon's Band of very inspired and gifted poets, poet-preachers and liturgists began their work, which was to prove as productive as it was infectious (for many, in any case). They were primarily from the NHK, although not exclusively so, difficult as that was for some to believe. For instance, the NHK professor A.F.N. Lekkerkerker (1913-1972) wrote in 1961, "We may assume that the GKN is not yet ready for a modernised Order III for the celebration of the Lord's Supper (*a liturgical formula*)."[8] Yet in 1966 the GKN came out with a number of relatively strongly modernised, clearly catholicising orders of worship, with an accompanying commentary. The eucharistic prayer in the Lord's Supper celebration has one preface which is built upon the Song of the Servant in Phil. 2,6-11. The congregation sings a Dutch translation of the adaptation of the Sanctus by the Anglican missionary bishop R. Heber (1783-1826), "Holy, Holy, Holy! Lord God Almighty!", to the tune by John B. Dykes (1823-1876). The Benedictus is, however, absent. The Agnus Dei can be sung in unrhymed form. In practice it is generally replaced by a rhymed hymn which can not really be termed an Agnus Dei, but does exude a strong sense of sin and grace.

In 1974 the GKN's worship supplement first appeared. This would appear again in 1981 in a revised version in a later, more ecumenical stage. But the inclusion of a Sanctus *and* Benedictus was already new in 1974. These were spoken or even sung, to a melody from Luther's German Mass. To put it in other words: the Reformation fear that the words "Blessed is he that cometh" would conjure up the suggestion of a real consecration had been conquered. In the NHK counterpart though, also published as a supplement, a rhymed version by Willem Barnard (b. 1920) was offered here, to be sung to the tune of Psalm 118 from the sixteenth century Geneva psalter (Louis Bourgeois *cum suis*).

Meanwhile, the GKN supplement also offered the possibility of singing an anamnestic acclamation, in this case that by Huub Oosterhuis (b. 1933) and Bernard Huijbers (b. 1922). As an alternative for the

[8] DE JONG: *Ordening van dienst* 195. Italics A. Lekkerkerker.

sung Agnus Dei, a rhymed version by G. Split (1917-1994) is suggested, which had already been included as hymn 188 in the *Liedboek voor de Kerken*[9] that had appeared in 1973. But note carefully: with all these developments in the direction of a catholic Lord's Supper liturgy, there was no movement toward an entirely sung eucharistic prayer.

2.2. 'De Adem van het jaar'

Nor was that the case in the important 1968 publication by the liturgists who once called themselves the "Adem van het jaar-groep."[10] Their names, and where they worked, are familiar to scholars in the field. Among them were the poets/writers W. Barnard, P. Elderenbosch (b. 1921), G. Overbosch (1919-2001), J. van der Werf (1926-1979) and others, including some from Roman Catholic backgrounds such as H. Oosterhuis and T. Naastepad (1921-1996). The places where they worked included Rozendaal, Amsterdam (the Maranathakerk and various other places), Amersfoort, Rotterdam Arauna, Utrecht's Domkerk and Zaandam's Ecumenical Workplace. These are names and places of yore – and to some extent of today still, next to other names and places that, fortunately, took hold. They have been termed "liturgical incubators."[11] We might add, incubators that proved very productive.

The 1968 publication, mentioned above, was entitled *Proeve van een Oecumenisch Ordinarium* (Specimen of an ecumenical *ordinarium*),[12] and appeared as number 36 in the series *Mededelingen van de Prof. dr G. van der Leeuw – Stichting*. This was the first source to include all the songs which form regular parts of the liturgy, in five musical settings by Freek Houtkoop, Bernard Huijbers, Frits Mehrtens (1922-1975), Ignace de Sutter (1911-1988) and Willem Vogel, together with a number of eucharistic prayers. Among the striking elements are:

[9] The *Liedboek voor de Kerken* is the official hymnal of the Dutch Reformed Church, the Reformed Churches in the Netherlands, the Evangelical Lutheran Church in the Kingdom of the Netherlands, the Remonstrant Brotherhood and the General Mennonite Society.

[10] During the 1960s new hymns were published in the series entitled *De Adem van het jaar* (The breath of the year).

[11] P. OSKAMP: *Liturgische broedplaatsen* (Kampen 1973).

[12] *Proeve van een Oecumenisch Ordinarium* (Amsterdam 1968).

(1) The rejection of any sort of rhymed version of the Sanctus/Benedictus (including Luther's "Isaiah the prophet...").
(2) The near rejection of a spoken or sung anamnestic acclamation, which is labelled as "to a certain degree disruptive."
(3) The objections to a sung Agnus Dei accompanying the breaking of the bread. This remarkable decision is justified as follows: "Through the identification of the bread and sacrificial lamb, that is to say through the increasingly more emphatically affirmed theories about a 'repetition without blood' of the sacrifice on Golgotha, a concentration on this theophany, on this mystery of faith that can be touched with the hands, has occurred, against which a serious objection most decidedly can be made."

Was it their choice, then, to leave out the Agnus Dei entirely? If the worst comes to the worst, this part should be sung, but then "as a congregational song during the final preparations for the eucharistic fellowship." A hymn such as Barnard's "Als Koning opgetreden," based on Revelations 19,6-10 and found in the *Liedboek voor de Kerken* as number 112, was, in this view, preferable.

It is however the song from the famous section from the *Didache* that is really recommended in the ecumenical *ordinarium.* That is an interesting development, which continues in the beautifully published, colourful congregational booklet *Onze hulp.*[13] For the rest, here the Agnus Dei and the blessing from the *Didache* stand one after the other deliberately, separated only by the passing of the peace, and not in opposition to each other. This liturgical publication, *Onze hulp*, is primarily significant ecumenically: it was published cooperatively by the NHK and GKN worship commissions. The respective Synods released it for use in the churches. Henceforth the two main streams of the Dutch Reformation *in liturgicis* would continue to advance collectively along the path of liturgy, though also in ever greater dialogue and cooperation with the ELK. In addition to diverse texts for the different rubrics of the whole celebration, there were nearly 30 eucharistic prayers provided, with four musical settings for the regularly included songs (Frits Mehrtens, Ignace de Sutter, Willem Vogel I and II), all of which had by then been tried out in various places. There was no sung

[13] Prof. dr G. van der Leeuw-Stichting (ed.), *"Onze hulp", een gemeenteboekje* (Amsterdam 1978).

anamnestic acclamation. In one of the services by Vogel the combination of the Agnus Dei and the Blessing from the *Didache* indeed was entirely sung.

It must be noted that the liturgist H. Wegman (1930-1996) criticised the rather stringent rejection of the Agnus Dei in the *Oecumenisch Ordinarium*, in which he was presumably right. It was, Wegman suggested, a misconception to think that in this acclamation bread and wine are lauded as autonomous "things."[14] In turn, Wegman was in error when he suggested that *Onze hulp* too still retained this rejection. That is not the case, as we have seen above. All this becomes particularly interesting in the light of what my colleague G. Rouwhorst (b. 1951) has convincingly argued with regard to the probably "double" origin of the Lord's Supper celebration in the early Church. There is reason to believe that the "*Didache* line" and the "Agnus Dei line" did not coincide from the very beginning.[15] Although this double source is not identical with it, in its turn it does touch upon the difference between the "line of the synagogue" and the "line of the upper room."[16] A peculiar place and function for the *Didache* liturgy, with its accent on praise and breaking of bread, as the celebration of a house community, thereby finally comes into sight.[17] In this connection, I would point out here already that the new service book of the Dutch Reformed Churches has included this liturgy as one of the eucharistic prayers; see further below.

In the sources mentioned above, there has been no suggestion of an entirely sung eucharistic prayer. Certainly, in some places the practise of a sung eucharistic prayer was already observed in this period. The liturgical settings where this occurred however continued to be exceptions. As far as that goes, suspicions piled up that they were elitist. To my mind, that was in fact the case: without "elitist" experiments (or even here and there traditions already) of this sort, we would never make any progress in the church! Nevertheless, it indeed remains a challenge to familiarise the whole of the church with a form of celebration which

[14] H. WEGMAN: Het tafelgebed van de vroeg-christelijke gemeente (originally 1992), in IDEM: *Voor de lange duur. Bijdragen over liturgie en spiritualiteit* (Baarn 1999) 295-303, p. 302.

[15] G. ROUWHORST: *De viering van de eucharistie in de vroege kerk* (Utrecht 1992).

[16] N.A. SCHUMAN: Vertrekpunten vertakkingen, in P. OSKAMP & N.A. SCHUMAN (eds.): *De weg van de liturgie. Tradities, achtergronden, praktijk* (Zoetermeer 1998^2) 23-51, esp. 30-31.

[17] WEGMAN: Het tafelgebed van de vroeg-christelijke gemeente 303.

includes music and the Muses in general. An important step in this direction was the Lutheran supplement from 1988, already mentioned. In addition to the order of service and *ordinarium* of 1955, the *ordinarium* of Willem Vogel reappears here, with a sung dialogue for the preface and the possibility of a sung institution. In addition, two "Liedmissen" are suggested. For the songs included in the service, the second of these deliberately makes exclusive use of the *Liedboek voor de Kerken*, that was by now being used in various churches.

2.3. Towards a new Reformed Service book

Thus, after the ecclesiastically sanctioned supplements and the somewhat less formal proposals such as those of the ecumenical *ordinarium* and *Onze hulp*, we arrive at the *Dienstboek – een proeve. Schrift, Maaltijd, Gebed* (Service book: a trial. Scripture, Lord's Supper, Prayer) that appeared in 1998.[18] Although this servicebook is still a 'trial', it is clear that in this publication almost fifty years of liturgical movement and liturgical creativity have come together, with a strong theological and/or liturgical pluriformity. The new service book provides a large number of eucharistic prayers, with a series that affords variants for the church year only in the preface and the post-Sanctus, and sometimes in the epiclesis. With regard to the music that is a regular part of the service, there are seven different *ordinaria* provided. In addition one finds two proposals for a "Liedmis." Classic hymns based on scripture (often in versions by Luther) appear in the first of these as the Sanctus and Agnus Dei.

It is interesting to see that, as is briefly mentioned above, the Praise or Blessing from the *Didache* is included here as an independent eucharistic prayer. It can be sung in its entirety in the setting by Willem Vogel, in unison.[19] In addition the *Dienstboek* offers five other sung eucharistic prayers. Most of these are also included in text form in the series of eucharistic prayers. These are the following texts and settings as found in the section "Liturgical Hymns" of the *Dienstboek*: "Gij louter licht" (Thou pure light), by Sytze de Vries (b. 1945) and Willem Vogel; "Gezegend is uw Naam" (Your Name is a source of blessing) by Nico Vlaming (b. 1955) and Aart de Kort (b. 1962); "Van alle dagen deze

[18] *Dienstboek. Een proeve. Schrift, Maaltijd, Gebed* (Zoetermeer 1998).

[19] The setting in parts for multiple voices is found in *Onze hulp* 70-72.

morgen" (Of all days this morning), by Bart Robbers (b. 1941) and Paul Schollaert; "Kom ons bevrijden" (Come, and rescue us!) by Niek Schuman (b. 1936) and Jan Pasveer (b. 1933); and "Gij die weet wat in mensen omgaat" (Thou who knowest the thoughts of men), by Huub Oosterhuis and Bernard Huijbers, which is not included in the series of textual eucharistic prayers.

It is worthwhile to say somewhat more about the eucharistic prayer "Kom ons bevrijden." This prayer was used many times in the Papenpad congregation in Zaandam (in the Old Catholic[20] church), and later in the Ecumenical Workplace, Zaandam, a congregation which could be characterised as being at the same time liturgically rather high church and rather low in its conception of ecclesiastical office. It was also included as a eucharistic prayer in the local song collection of the Good Shepherd Parish in Amsterdam in 1979. I will briefly indicate five of its characteristics:

(1) It is constructed in the traditional manner from the dialogue to the Agnus Dei. It is sung alternatively by the celebrant and the congregation, whereby the congregation is always divided into two different groups of voices, for instance women and men, or choir and all.
(2) The *Salvator mundi* recurs throughout the whole eucharistic prayer: "Saviour of the world, come set us free." This is also the only part sung in harmony.
(3) The institution narrative is sung in recitation tone, the narrative section in G, the words of institution in the even higher B-flat.
(4) The circle is actually closed in the sung anamnestic acclamation; it is composed as a partial canon. Directly hereafter follow prayers of supplication in which the whole world is involved in this *communio*. These prayers are sung in recitation tone, deliberately beginning with low C.
(5) Quite in keeping with this, the prayer from the *Didache* for "ingathering from the great dispersion" also receives a place here.

Hopefully in the preceding pages something has become visible of what we could call the spirituality of the Reformation Lord's Supper cel-

[20] The Old Catholic Church in the Netherlands arose in 1723 as a separation from the Roman Catholic Church.

ebration, and its eucharistic prayers. On the one side, the development sketched here has been somewhat laborious. Without too much difficulty, one can point to the compromises coming forth from theology and church policy or, reversely, the moments in which no compromises were possible. Yet, on the other side, there has been a constant which has run through the whole. I am referring to the attempt to really involve the "people of God" in the liturgy of the Lord's Supper. In practice this has often undeniably resulted in liturgical patchwork. In particular, time and again it has always been very difficult to introduce unrhymed songs into the regular service music. Very often therefore it has been necessary to fall back on favourite hymns from the *Liedboek* or elsewhere. Otherwise it would all too quickly be only the choir who would be singing! Thus in the end, in spite of all the liturgical material, we come out with a sort of "Liedmis." That can be very worthwhile. But then one must certainly take more care that there is a measure of continuity in the sort of language and music used than is generally the case now. At the same time it is true that only by this process of gradual change can something of a communality in diversity grow in Reformation praxis.

The latter can be illustrated by the recent *Dienstboek*. At its presentation, on October 31, 1998, the diversity of Dutch Reformed traditions which is shown by the *Dienstboek* was stressed. This variety of shape becomes visible in the diversity of all sorts of texts for the Lord's Supper, of which some have a rather celebratory, and others a rather didactic character. The didactic order uses the Lord's Supper formula from the Dutch Reformed tradition or a version of Calvin's prayer for the Lord's Supper, in which those continuing in sin are instructed not to come to the Lord's Supper, but at the same time all present are summoned to come to the table "where Jesus Christ himself so lovingly calls us through his Word." For the celebratory order there are the series of eucharistic prayers already discussed, most spoken, some sung. Here, to my understanding, an open account from the Reformation is finally paid, properly and with reason: the thankful blessing of all the acts of God. For the rest, the third track is new: the order of a Lord's Supper liturgy in which a not too heavily accentuated didactic component enters into a meaningful relationship with a celebratory component. For that the Praise from the *Didache* is used again.

3. Celebrating the Lord's Supper: the Psalms

It may be interesting to see what songs were used in the traditional Calvinist celebration of the Lord's Supper as an expression of the participation of the entire congregation in the liturgy. While on rare occasions a "Biblical" hymn was allowed, the vast majority of songs represented were psalms. I take as an example the instructions from the GKN Synod at Middelburg in 1933. What sort of psalms are recommended by the Synod of 1933 for the celebration of the Lord's Supper itself? One might expect that the genre of penitential psalms would predominate, of psalms in which the "enemies of the Lord" (in this case the impenitent, sent away according to the traditional "exhortation to self-examination") were dispelled and dispersed. Surprisingly enough, that is not the case. Certainly, Psalm 130 is on the list. But here the congregation sings not only contritely, "out of the depths," but more centrally confesses "I wait for the Lord with all my soul... My soul waits for the Lord more eagerly than watchmen for the morning." Is that not precisely very meet and right and fitting for the Lord's Supper?

The other psalms suggested strengthen the impression that the eucharistic spirituality here is expressed primarily in the theme of "being a guest of the Eternal." For example, there is Psalm 84, in fact a hymn on the intimacy of the house of the Lord:

> How dear is thy dwelling-place, thou Lord of Hosts!
> I pine, I faint with longing for the courts of the Lord's temple;
> my whole being cries out with joy to the living God.
> (Ps. 84,1-2 NEB)

Liturgically, the inclusion of Psalms 23 and 42 is especially noteworthy. These are precisely the psalms, in which waters stream richly, that were familiar from time immemorial as songs of faith for the accompaniment of people in their first and last rites of passage, both at baptismal celebrations and funeral services. Between the two threshold rituals stands then the repeated avowal of trust in God as shepherd and as source of light and truth.

The choice of suggested psalms for the Preparatory Service (on the preceding Sunday) is also remarkable. In the "classic" Reformed tradition this Preparation still has a prominent place, generally not more than four times a year. Now, the psalms advised for this are those which indeed can encourage examination of one's conscience. Psalm 139 could be taken as a first example, with its emphasis on divine omnipresence and its closing prayer:

> Examine me, O God, and know my thoughts
> test me, and understand my misgivings.
> Watch lest I follow any path that grieves thee;
> guide me in the everlasting ways.
> (Ps. 139,23-24 NEB)

The twin psalms 15 and 24 are a second example. In both songs the central question is

O Lord, who may lodge in thy tabernacle?
Who may dwell on thy holy mountain?
(Ps. 15,1 NEB)

Who may go up the mountain of the Lord?
And who may stand in his holy place?
(Ps. 24,3 NEB)

It is exactly these accents in the Preparation for the Lord's Supper that can lead to a certain gloominess, if not to the outright avoidance of the Lord's Supper. That is their negative side. The positive side is however the critical, prophetic element that lies within them, fundamentally nothing other than the summons from Jesus to go first to your brother or sister and be reconciled with them, and only then go to the altar (Matt. 5,23-24). This choice of psalms emphasizes that a noncommittal celebration of the Lord's Supper, without any obligation on our part, is an impossibility.

There are no suggestions made in the *Liedboek voor de Kerken* any more for the Preparation, although there are still suggestions for the Lord's Supper celebration itself. Now there are many more songs on the list, such as the rhymed version of the Nunc Dimittis, and still various psalms. In addition to psalms "out of the depths" such as Psalms 22 and 130, and in addition to the "water and bread" psalms mentioned above such as Psalms 23 and 42, the presence of Psalm 118 is striking. That is, after all, the psalm from which the Benedictus is derived: "Blessed be he that comes in the name of the Lord!" One can ask how many people are still aware that this is the origin of that superb line, but in fact it is. Psalm 118 sings of how someone who was completely written off, even rejected, returns gloriously to the temple, in order to enter there through the "gates of righteousness." It is a song of wonderment, as impressive as it is meaningful. The very earliest Jewish-Christian community found in this song the expression of the deepest messianic secret.[21]

4. Conclusion: towards a "Psalm Mass"

That brings me finally to my argument for a "Psalm Mass (Psalmmis)" in addition to the eucharistic prayers discussed above, spoken or sung, and in addition to the two-fold "Liedmis" included in the *Dienstboek*. Possibly precisely a Lord's Supper celebration in the form of a "Psalm Mass" could build a bridge between the ecumenical-Protestant line on the one side and the classic-Reformed line on the other. Two opposites that previously seemed to avoid each other can perhaps become neighbours again – indeed, thanks to psalms! I offer the following thoughts on this suggestion:

(1) The thematic structure of very many psalms, and furthermore of many groups of psalms, can be viewed as the ur-structure of all liturgy: that of *kyrie* and *gloria*, often enough in reverse order. One may see this structure, for instance, in Ps. 40,9-11 and 12-13:

> In the great assembly I have proclaimed what is right,
> I do not hold back my words, as thou knowest, O Lord.
> I have not kept thy goodness hidden in my heart;
> I have proclaimed thy faithfulness and saving power,
> and not concealed thy unfailing love and truth
> from the great assembly.
> Thou, O Lord, dost not withhold thy tender care from me;
> thy unfailing love and truth for ever guard me.
>
> For misfortunes beyond counting press on me from all sides;
> my iniquities have overtaken me, and my sight fails;
> they are more than the hairs of my head,
> and my courage fails me.
> Show me favour, O Lord, and save me;
> hasten to help me, O Lord.
> (NEB)

[21] See also N.A. Schuman: Het spoor van een lied van verbazing, in Idem: *Verbonden voor het leven. Bijbeltheologische opstellen* (Delft 1988) 23-60.

(2) The range of individual themes of the psalms can without too much difficulty be called upon to express an equal range of visions and experiences of faith. As well as the lament – sometimes even an indictment – there are praise and astonishment. Great visions of the meeting between truth and righteousness are as a matter of course compatible with intimacy like that found in Psalm 25:

> The Lord confides his purposes to those who fear him,
> and his covenant is theirs to know.
> My eyes are ever on the Lord,
> who alone can free my feet from the net.
> (Ps. 25,14-15 NEB)

The bridge which can connect the one side with the other lies in such poetic language. Here one learns what it really means to cross the Jordan, barely make it to the shore, to enter the house of the Lord to take sanctuary like a small bird, and to wait for the Living One "more eagerly than watchmen for the morning."

(3) By way of the psalms one can also on the one hand arrive at the explicit acknowledgement of "the Jewish roots of Christian worship,"[22] and, on the other hand, an open and critical dialogue with the other sons of Abraham and Isaac. After all, the earliest generations of Christians, from among the circumcised and from among the nations, fathomed and bore witness to the messianic contours of the cross and resurrection precisely with the help of the psalms. In doing so, they joined in a process of messianic interpretation that had gotten under way well before Christ.[23] They sought the "Christ of the Scriptures" in the psalms – or to put it in other terms, the words of the psalms helped them to fathom the depths of the messianic way of cross and resurrection. Thus, when all is said and done, I could imagine a liturgy of Scripture, Lord's Supper and Prayer in the form of a "Psalm Mass" – by definition, largely sung – in part rhymed, with the traditional Genevan tunes, in part unrhymed, with the assistance of the newly composed psalms by

[22] R. BOON: *De joodse wortels van de christelijke eredienst* (Amsterdam 1970).

[23] See especially G. BRAULIK: Christologisches Verständnis der Psalmen – schon im Alten Testament?, in IDEM *et al.* (eds.): *Biblische Theologie und gesellschaftlicher Wandel* (Freiburg 1993) 57-86.

Piet Oussoren (text) and Gert Oost (music).[24] In closing, several suggestions follow here.

(4) In addition to psalm fragments that are already determined by the liturgical calendar, cheerful psalms such as 149 or 84 should function in the opening ritual. There are fine elements in the latter of a real threshold ritual, that could be used with further aid from the ancient Psalm 43 (earlier part of the priest's prayers at the foot of the altar!) or Psalm 65:

> We owe thee praise, O God, in Zion;
> thou hearest prayer, vows shall be paid to thee.
> (Ps. 65,1-2 NEB)

Psalms like 130 and 139 can powerfully put into words the personal prayer for forgiveness. A song like Psalm 80 expressively calls for renewal for a world in need:

> Restore us, O God,
> and make thy face shine upon us that we may be saved.
> (Ps. 80,3 NEB)

(5) The psalms during the service of the Word, as responsive psalms and as sung after the sermon, will naturally be selected with the season of the liturgical year in mind.

(6) Psalm 141 has traditionally recommended itself for the prayer of intercession:

> O Lord, I call to thee, come quickly to my aid;
> listen to my cry when I call to thee.
> Let my prayer be like incense duly set before thee
> and my raised hands like the evening sacrifice.
> (Ps. 141,1-2 NEB)

In the service of the Lord's Supper, Psalms 98 and 118 could function excellently as hymns after the preface. That is obvious for Psalm 118, with the Benedictus in verse 26. But also Psalm 98, with its accent on the divine kingship *à la* the vision of the prophet in Isaiah 6 (with the Sanctus), comes close to this:

[24] These strophe psalms are sung on a typical chant-psalmody, which is directly based on the classic Genevan melody of the rhymed psalms.

Acclaim the Lord, all men on earth,
break into songs of joy, sing psalms.
Sing psalms in the Lord's honour with the harp,
with the harp and with music of the psaltery.
With trumpet and echoing horn
acclaim the presence of the Lord our king.
(Ps. 98,4-6 NEB)

Psalm 80 could serve as the Agnus Dei:

Hear us, O shepherd of Israel,
who leadest Joseph like a flock of sheep.
Show thyself, thou that art throned on the cherubim,
to Ephraim and to Benjamin.
Rouse thy victorious might from slumber,
come to our rescue.
(Ps. 80,1-2 NEB)

The communion, and the whole of the service, could be closed with the psalm that has attended those receiving baptism and communicants throughout the centuries:

The Lord is my shepherd; I shall want nothing.
He makes me lie down in green pastures,
and leads me beside the waters of peace;
he renews life within me,
and for his name's sake guides me in the right path.
Even though I walk through a valley as dark as death
I fear no evil, for thou art with me,
thy staff and thy crook are my comfort.

Thou spreadest a table for me in the sight of my enemies;
thou hast richly bathed my head with oil,
and my cup runs over.
Goodness and love unfailing, these will follow me
all the days of my life
and I shall dwell in the house of the Lord
my whole life long.
(Ps. 23 NEB)

Anton Vernooij

MUSIC AND LITURGY IN MOVEMENT CHURCH MUSIC IN THE NETHERLANDS FROM 1865 TO 2000

1. Introduction

At international conferences and in contacts with colleagues from other countries I am often asked to describe the contemporary liturgical music of the Netherlands. People seem to be particularly interested in the background of developments surrounding and following the Second Vatican Council, and especially in the background and role of the Amsterdam Study Group for Vernacular Liturgy, with which the names of the poet Huub Oosterhuis (b. 1933) and the composer Bernard Huijbers (b. 1922) are profoundly linked. The work of these two in particular has become known widely outside the Netherlands.[1] It would appear that both because of the language barrier and because of its often selective choice of subjects, the existing literature in Dutch does not optimally answer the questions being asked about these topics, while much of the non-Dutch literature is characterised by a sometimes superficial analysis of developments in the Netherlands.[2]

[1] A number of liturgical books by Huub Oosterhuis have been translated. A selection: *Ganz nah ist dein Wort* and *Du bist der Atem meiner Lieder* (1976), both published by Herder/Vienna. In 1989 Patmos/Düsseldorf published *Um Recht und Frieden*. A considerable amount of music from the Amsterdam Study Group was published in the USA by North American Liturgy Sources. In England Tony Barr (Jabulani Music) has set up an "Amsterdam" centre. The German language song collection *Gotteslob* (1975) includes seven song texts by Oosterhuis and 3 tunes by Huijbers. Lehrhaus und Liturgie Osnabrück has brought out three cd's with songs by Oosterhuis: *Der mich trug*, *Mitten unter uns* and *Licht und Atem*. The cd's *Wake your Power* and *Turn your Heart* were put out by the Oregon Catholic Press.

[2] J. Coleman: *The evolution of Dutch Catholicism 1954-1974* (Berkeley 1978); W. Damberg: *Abschied vom Milieu? Katholizismus im Münster und in den Niederlanden 1945-1980* (Paderborn 1997); W. Frijhoff: Reflexions sur la transformation du catholicisme hollandais 1960-1970, in A. Dierkens (ed.): *Le libéralisme religieux* (Bruxelles 1992) 111-126; W. Goddijn: Some religious developments in the Netherlands

I have seized upon the publication of this book, *Liturgy and Muse*, as the occasion to make good on the promise that I have so often made, and will use this study to sketch the origins and further development of the "Dutch model".[3]

My story begins at a time in which a new era in liturgy dawned, not only for the Netherlands but also for many other countries in Europe, namely with the growth of the Liturgical Movement, approximately from the middle of the nineteenth century. In the Netherlands this new development also coincided both with a fundamental reorganisation of Roman Catholic church life, including the restoration in 1853 of the episcopal hierarchy, which had been lost around 1580 as a consequence of the Reformation, and with the beginning of a general "Catholic revival", as it has been called by the historian L. Rogier (1894-1974).[4] It must be further added that the development of liturgical music in the Netherlands can only be understood in terms of the renaissance of church music in the wake of Cecilianism, the fresh wind that blew in from neighbouring Germany, and which was formally affirmed in the decrees of the Provincial Synod of Utrecht, held in 1865. This explains the choice of the year 1865 in the subtitle of this study.

This study will chiefly be concerned with the backgrounds for the developments. From the course of the general Western European current of the Liturgical Movement, attention will be given to its specifically Dutch facets. Obviously, Catholic life in the Netherlands has developed in an ambience and according to a process of growth unique to itself. By this ambience, I have in mind Calvinism, which spread through the Netherlands at the end of the sixteenth century. The Catholic revival in the Netherlands, including the revival in church music, was strongly defined by the pluriform Dutch religious constellation. This has led to church music in the Dutch Roman Catholic tradition being

1947-1979, in *Social Compass* 30 (1983) 409-424; T. OOSTVEEN: Le catholicisme néerlandais dans les années soixante-dix, in *Septentrion* (1979) 5-13; H.G. SURMUND: Von der Polarisierung zum Dialog. Zur Situation der katholischen Kirche in den Niederlanden, in A. LOHE and O. MÜLLER: *Gelebtes Europa. Nachbar Niederlande* (Aachen 1996) 146-161.

[3] A term coined in Germany.

[4] L.J. ROGIER and N. DE ROOY: *In vrijheid herboren: katholiek Nederland 1853-1953* ('s-Gravenhage 1953).

characterised on the one hand by self-centred devotionalism, a cherished legacy from the period of repression under Calvinism (the conventicle period), and on the other by a new élan, which was both self-confident and triumphalist and militant.

The final section of this article is devoted not to an evaluation of the past of liturgical music in the Netherlands, but to a consideration of the qualities of liturgical music at the beginning of the 21st century. While the Dutch situation remains the point of departure for this, it will here be seen chiefly as part of European culture as a whole.

2. The European context

The development of church music in the Netherlands took place within the currents of the wider Liturgical Movement in Europe, which strove for a revitalisation of liturgical materials. With regard to church music, its two fundamental pillars, Gregorian plainsong and polyphony, were sought out. These developments took place primarily in France and Germany. In the Netherlands the restoration of Gregorian song would ultimately occur in the French spirit, while the renewal of polyphonic music was based on a firmly German foundation.[5]

2.1. France: Dom Guéranger and Solesmes

Often the significance of Dom Prosper Guéranger (1805-1875) and the abbey of Solesmes, which he restored to life, is thought to be limited to a fundamental contribution to the restoration of Gregorian song. Guéranger's efforts to have the Church let go of the national (neo-gallican) liturgy and return to the spirit and content of the one true liturgy, that of the Church of Rome with its "unsurpassed balance between sense and performance, between belief and experience: a liturgy in spirit and in truth, guaranteed by the Spirit and one around the Pope, the leader of the Church",[6] were no less influential. Further, the abbot

[5] Until the introduction of the 1908 *Graduale Romanum*, what were termed "Mechelen books" (from Mechelen, Belgium) were widely used.

[6] H.A.J. Wegman: *Christian worship in East and West. A study guide tot liturgical history* (New York 1985) 246. Cf. P. Raedts: De katholieken en de Middeleeuwen. Prosper Guéranger OSB (1805-1875) en de eenheid van de liturgie, in R. Stuip & C. Vellekoop (eds.): *De Middeleeuwen in de negentiende eeuw* (Hilversum 1996) 87-109.

strove for an exulted form of worship, at the expense of a more popular devotionality. His ideal was a liturgy, thought out and celebrated by monks in an old, solemn, courtly style, with exalted Gregorian chant as the authentic song repertoire. In his manual for Christian worship, the liturgist Herman Wegman (1930-1996) proposes that the Gregorian performance which was achieved, the ceremonial style in which the liturgy was celebrated, the strictly ordered, solemn *officium divinum* which made the liturgy à la Guéranger so exalted, made it inaccessible for other believers: distant, celebrated by monks in the choir. It was a liturgy to listen to, to watch, a liturgy to smell, as incense burned daily.[7] An important source by which "Solesmes" spread through the Netherlands was the Benedictine abbey in Oosterhout, North Brabant, founded by Wisges in 1907.

Seen purely from the perspective of church music, the spirit of Guéranger really penetrated the Netherlands only in the long term. At first, it was obstructed by the spirit of Cecilianism (see §2.2). Moreover, Guéranger's influence was tempered by another current in the Liturgical Movement, which likewise would have no small influence on the development of church music in the Netherlands. We must at this point particularly mention the pastoral-liturgical attitude of the liturgist Dom Lambert Beauduin (1873-1960), and the influential studies on the *Mysterienlehre* and the *Mysterien-gegenwart* by Dom Odo Casel (1886-1948), and the name of Romano Guardini, who opened the eyes of so many to the irreplaceable value of the style and spirit of the liturgy. His book *Vom Geist der Liturgie* was also a bestseller in the Netherlands.[8]

The mention of Dom Beauduin's name raises the question of possible Belgian influence on church music in the Netherlands. This question is all the more important, in view of the many positive developments which took place in the field there, for instance in the archdiocese of Mechelen in the second half of the nineteenth century. For example, already in 1879 the important Diocesan School for Church Music had been opened in Mechelen by J. Lemmens. Especially in the area of the restoration of Gregorian music (the "Mechelen books" mentioned above) Belgium was far in the lead, certainly as compared with

[7] WEGMAN: *Christian worship* 247.

[8] H. WEGMAN: Liturgie in Rooms-Katholiek Nederland van 1892-1981: gingen de luiken open?, in *Hendrik Andriessen en het tijdperk der ontluiking* (Redactieraad kerkmuziek & liturgie, Utrecht 1993) 23-43.

the Netherlands, but even compared with France or Germany. These Belgian editions were being introduced in the Netherlands until, in the years after about 1880, the spirit of the church music dominant there began to blow across the borders from Germany. But, as far as is known, few (or no) students from the Netherlands were trained in Mechelen in the years before 1925, when professional training in church music began in Utrecht (see §3.3), while Dutch church musicians were indeed being trained in Aachen and Regensburg in Germany.

2.2. Cecilianism

Nineteenth century Cecilianism was of even greater importance for the development of Dutch church music than was the movement of Dom Guéranger.[9] Cecilianism owes its name to the Allgemeiner Cäcilien-Verein, founded at the annual national gathering of German Roman Catholics at Bamburg in 1868 by F.X. Haberl (1840-1910), although in terms of import it had been active in Germany earlier. Cecilianism was a reform movement that set for itself the goals of restoring the true nature of church music and once again inseparably linking it with liturgical activity. The centre of Cecilianism would become the city of Regensburg. Unlike Guéranger, Cecilianism did not seek the sources of the liturgy in the old Church (i.e., in the Roman monastic liturgy and Gregorian song of the High Middle Ages), but rather where, according to views influenced by Romanticism, the true source of Church life should be sought: Rome of the sixteenth and seventeenth century. In 1871 the Regensburg publisher Friedrich Pustet reprinted the 1614 *Editio Medicaea* as the most authentic source for Gregorian song. Toward the end of the century, Solesmes and Regensburg would increasingly dispute each other's views with regard to Gregorian song. However, even more than the restoration of Gregorian song, Cecilianism sought the restoration of polyphonic church music. The ideal frame of reference for this was sixteenth century Roman practice in church music, which was identified with the person and compositions of Giovanni Pierluigi da Palestrina (1525-1594). Cecilianism, for the rest, was more than just a movement in church music. Church music was seen as the means par excellence for bringing the 'faithful' back to the Church

[9] Cf. W. KIRSCH: Caecilianismus, in *Die Musik in Geschichte und Gegenwart* (Kassel 1995) Sachteil II, 318-326.

and church culture, and combatting all developments tending toward individualism. Paul Krutschek expressed this goal as follows: "Wir Cäcilianer sind die kirchenmusikalischen Jesuiten, gegen Irrtum und Bosheit kämpfend für die Vorschrifte der Kirche."[10]

The great significance of Cecilianism for Dutch Catholic life in general and for church music in particular is closely linked with the Catholic revival already mentioned. Cecilianism found a rich seedbed in the religious-artistic climate which prevailed in the Netherlands, in which, for instance, the Neo-Gothic architectural style would also flourish. Cecilianism was therefore not merely a reaction to the deterioration of nineteenth century church music, and particularly to the secularisation, individualism and tendency toward the use of soloists in musical expression, and to the increasing independence of the music from liturgical activity; it was no less than a conservative ecclesiastical answer to the aesthetic complexity of the cultural developments of its time. Cecilianism, like the Neo-Gothic architectural style, was "born with its head looking backwards", as L.J. Rogier put it.[11] What was wrong with the spirit of both Cecilianism and Neo-Gothicism was, according to him, that their proponents "sounded the alarm in the name of orthodoxy in a stock fashion, as soon as modern art and its aberrations tried to penetrate the sanctuaries".[12] Until far into the twentieth century, Dutch church music was Cecilian in spirit.

The Cecilian church music style was expressed in simplicity of means, transparent musical structures, unity of rhythm, restraint in dynamics, and in a musical idiom which appealed directly to the listener. Liturgical texts were also declared to be untouchable. The organ was put forward as the only real liturgical instrument. It served almost exclusively as the accompaniment for sung liturgical texts and congregational singing. Away, then, with the orchestra and *alternatimspel*! This last referred to a practice in which the organ all alone by itself took the place of one of the two groups that should have alternated in singing parts of the sung ordinary (Kyrie-Gloria-Agnus Dei) antiphonally.

Alas, in many respects the good intentions led to musical products that were aesthetically impoverished and of middling quality. At first masses and motets were imported to the Netherlands from Germany

[10] Quoted by Kirsch: Caecilianismus 321.
[11] L.J. ROGIER: *Katholieke herleving* ('s-Gravenhage 1956) 520.
[12] ROGIER: *Katholieke herleving* 520.

itself, among others pieces by a founder of the Cäcilienverein, Franz Xaver Witt (1834-1888), and by Michael Haller (1840-1915). Only later was something more uniquely Dutch to be heard, from the pens of composers like Johan Winnubst (1885-1934), from Utrecht, Philip Loots (1865-1916), from Haarlem, Willem Heydt (1858-1928), from Nijmegen, and Hubert Cuypers (1873-1960), from Amsterdam.

Finally, it was characteristic of Cecilianism that it was supported and led by priests of a Church which was becoming increasingly more clerical, and which had little or no eye (or ear) for modern religious thought in word or music. As is so often the case in history, their strict dogmatism was not as strictly followed by the people in the parishes.

3. Revitalisation of church music in the nineteenth century

3.1. The Provincial Synod of Utrecht, 1865

On March 4, 1853, by issuing the brief *Ex qua die* Pope Pius IX provided the Netherlands with full episcopal administration. It was a clear milestone in a phase of restoration and revitalisation of Dutch Catholicism. This important step was followed in 1865 with the Provincial Synod of Utrecht, at which the beginning of a new direction for church music too was confirmed. From a comparison of the provisions in the sixth chapter of its proceedings with those of the later Motu-Proprio *Tra le sollecitudini* (1903) from Pope Pius X, and with the stipulations of Pope Pius XI which were to come still later, it would seem that the action items regarding church music on the agenda of the Popes mentioned had already been put into words by the Utrecht Synod.[13] They all drew from the gushing fountainhead of Cecilianism.

Rogier has described the Synod of 1865 as "the apotheosis, the ostentatious closing act of the work of regulating, ordering and unravelling" that had to be done after the restoration of the Dutch episcopal hierarchy.[14] According to the Synod, Gregorian song is the proper music for the Church. Entirely in the Cecilian spirit, however, polyphonic music then should be composed according to the rules of Christian art, thus

[13] *Acta et decreta synodi provincialis Ultrajectensis* (St. Michielsgestel 1865).
[14] Rogier and De Rooy: *In vrijheid herboren* 204.

being characterised by gravity, dignity, purity and majesty. Profane melodies in the style of opera are reprehensible. Most important, the music must not awaken any feelings that are out of place in a church. It must be truly sung together, not screamed out together, as is so often the case. After all, the purpose of this church music is to quicken and nourish the piety of the believers, not to disrupt it. Songs in the vernacular are only permitted after the celebration, and the text of every song must be derived from antiphons or hymns recognised by the Church. Next, the song must be inspired by the spirit of the Church, and be either festive and productive of joy, or sorrowful, leading to repentance. Without the express permission of Church authorities, no other instrument than the organ may sound, and the organ may neither overwhelm the song nor offend the heart. The organ accompaniment must be stately in rhythm and tempo, subordinate to the liturgical actions, and most of all, may not serve the soloistic enjoyment of the organist. Women may not sing in the choir, not just because that is simply forbidden and conflicts with the dignity of church music, but also because it does not square with the religious sentiments of the faithful. Finally, it is set down that the singers must be pious, and that which they sing with the mouth must be confirmed by their works.[15]

3.2. The practice of church music

Behind the rules in the proceedings of the Utrecht Synod one can read a description of the general practice of church music at the time. Seen from the Cecilian perspective, the situation was rotten and deserving of censure. The Synod Fathers clearly show their distaste for the existing practice of predominant choral singing. I will permit myself to cite the witty and suggestive description of the repertoire of the better singing choirs, from an address by M.J.A. Lans (1845-1908), chairman of the newly-founded Dutch St. Gregory Association,[16] given in Antwerp in 1882:

[15] In September, 1924, a Provincial Council was held once again. It dealt with matters of ecclesiastical law, and the subject of church music was not on the agenda. See *Acta et decreta Concilii Provincialis Ultrajectensis* (St. Michelsgestel 1924).

[16] For this Association, see section 3.3.

> But I have not yet told you (...) of the very worst offense (...) You cannot call it bungling, it isn't even so good as that (...) I mean that stringing together, that pasting together, that knocking together (...) of liturgical texts to choruses and solos from oratorios, operas, folk songs, piano pieces and who knows what else – for instance, O Salutaris to "Mit Wurd' und Hoheit" from *Die Schöpfung*, or to "O Isis und Osiris" from *Die Zauberflöte*; or Jesu Redemptor to "Nun scheint in vollem Glanze" from *Die Schöpfung* (...) or Tantum Ergo to "Gott erhalte Franz den Kaiser" and... O Salutaris Hostia to "In diesen heil'gen Halle".
> The sacristy bell gives two-three strokes, and (...) the long awaited, the holy moment has come (...) How everything disposes to sobriety, how all inspires awe, how all breathes holiness! And at that moment (...) Do you hear it? (...) that unliturgical choir (...) it is busy tuning its instruments!! a..a..a... wheezes the organ, ching go the violins, chum the double bases, tluut tluut the flutes, tre tre the trumpets, boom the kettledrums and the big base drum (...) My God, am I still in your holy Temple? I've only heard that before at the concert, only at the opera! (...) Now they let fly: one, two three...Kyrie...what a racket! – Another Kyrie...still more racket! Ky..Ky..Ky..Ky..Kyrie..all the singers at the top of their lungs, all the instruments still much louder!....Boom.....Done! – Christe etc. (...) Act one of the symphony is finished.[17]

What kinds of things were they singing? In his book on church music in the Netherlands since the Reformation, Dr. L. Kat calls the second half of the nineteenth century the era of the great masses.[18] Until about 1875 these were those of Ludwig von Beethoven (1770-1827), Josef Haydn (1732-1809), Luigi Cherubini (1760-1842), J.B. van Bree (1801-1857) and J.W. Kalliwoda (1801-1866). The masses by Van Bree were, as somewhat later also those of J.J.H. Verhulst (1816-1891), J.J. Viotta (1814-1859), W.A. Smit (1804-1869) and G.A. Heinze (1820-1904), experienced as new, composed under the influence of the Liturgical Movement. From smaller choirs one long heard what are termed the Amsterdam and Louvain masses, of the eighteenth century, clearly written by amateurs for amateurs, and intended to imitate the great masses.[19] Their principle purpose was to be easily sung, while providing a range

[17] M.J.A. LANS: *Eeredienst en Toonkunst* (Leiden 1882) 55ff.

[18] A.I.M. KAT: *De geschiedenis der kerkmuziek in de Nederlanden sedert de hervorming* (Hilversum 1939) 178.

[19] P. BILLE: *Duodecim Missae et Missa pro defunctis, sequuntur quatuor antiphonae de beata Maria virgine, et viginti-quatuor modulamina, duarum vocum* (Leuven 1975).

of cheap effects. According to Kat, the works of L. Lambillotte (1796-1855), J. Vieuxbois (nineteenth century), J.M. d'Archambeau (1823-1899), J. van Paesschen (nineteenth century) and B.A. Potharst (nineteenth century) in general were of less quality than those of Verhulst and company, and handled the texts less adroitly than those of their northern colleagues.[20] Only toward the end of the century would the renewal reach the point, thanks to Cecilianism, that choirs really began to replace their cherished repertoire pieces with Mass ordinaria which would then hold out until the middle of the twentieth century. Examples of these are the masses by German Cecilians like M. Haller (1840-1915), I. Mitterer (1850-1924), J. Stehle (1839-1915) and P. Piel (1835-1904), and particularly the Italian Lorenzo Perosi (1872-1956). This improvement in quality was in part the result of the zeal of the St. Gregory Association, which in the first decades of its existence would devote itself to the new church music – in particular, for the motets and masses of Palestrina – in the Cecilian spirit par excellence. Outside the Mass – officially it was not permitted during Mass, or even after it was over – the people sang, generally loudly and assertively, during pilgrimages and gatherings of the Archconfraternity of the Holy Family or the Maria Congregation. On the occasion of a priest's or bishop's jubilee – or especially a Papal jubilee – the choir triumphantly sang out their Catholic identity in festive cantatas and motets.[21]

3.3. The Dutch St. Gregory Association

In terms of church music, the most important result of the Provincial Council was the founding of the Nederlandse St.-Gregoriusvereniging (NSGV, Dutch St. Gregory Association) in 1878. Since the beginning of the 1870s there had been choir groups started here and there in the diocese of Haarlem to promote Gregorian song. During the fourth quarter of the nineteenth century such groups would arise in all the other Dutch dioceses. From the example of such groups outside the Netherlands, they called themselves "Gregorian Associations" and, inspired by the Provincial Council in Utrecht and Cecilianism, took as their responsibility the local renewal of liturgical music. On December 27, 1874,

[20] KAT: *Geschiedenis der kerkmuziek* 178ff.

[21] A. VERNOOIJ: '...zal opwekken tot luide dank- en jubelkreten'. De priestercantate in Nederland van 1860 tot 1960, in *Jaarboek voor liturgie-onderzoek* 16 (2000) 235-258.

Nicolaas Andriessen, organist of the Haarlem cathedral church, and J.J. Graaf, secretary to the Bishop, succeeded in establishing a Gregorian Association for the city of Haarlem. The statutes of this Haarlem association consisted primarily of citations from the sixth chapter of the acts of the Synod. The magazine *Sint Gregoriusblad* was founded by a national committee of church musicians in 1876, and continues to appear down to this day. Subsequently, in February, 1878, the editors of this periodical founded a national association for church music, the Dutch St. Gregory Association, which was charged by the episcopacy with carrying out the Synod resolutions, and with oversight of church music in general. When founding the NSGV, the editors of the *Sint Gregoriusblad* who organised it had an eye on what was happening in other countries. Following the lead of the German Cäcilienverein, Dr. Jos. Satzmann had started a Cecilia Association in America in 1873. In 1876 Italy got its Associazione di S. Cecilia, through the later abbot G. Amelli. That same year, 1876, Nicolaus Donnelly founded a Gregorian Association in Ireland. That same name was taken by the organisations founded by Alfred Young in North America in 1877, by Canon Van Damme in Belgium in 1880, and in England in 1883.

4. After the turn of the century

4.1. Regeneration in the world Church

Undoubtedly the Motu-Proprio *Tra le sollecitudini* of Pope Pius X, written in the earliest days of his pontificate and dated November 22, 1903, was the most influential reaction to the developments in Western Europe which have been described above. The document is chiefly of importance because on the one hand it clearly and lucidly articulates what was wrong with church music as it was practised in the nineteenth century, and on the other hand because it was definitive for the further development of church music. According to the Pope this must be considered as an essential component (*parte integrante*) of the solemnly celebrated liturgy, and has as its purpose the glorification of God and the sanctification and edification of the believers. To the greatest extent possible it must have the characteristics of liturgy itself, namely *sanctity* with regard to both content and presentation, *beauty of form* so that it is *true art*, and *universality*. This last means that church music may never leave a bad impression anywhere in the world, in any culture. The qualities listed, which were also accepted criteria outside the Church in the nineteenth century, are especially to be found in Gregorian song, the peculiar song of the Roman Church. There this must again take a central place in the liturgy. One must again have the people sing Gregorian song, and thus permit them to actively take part again (*affinché i fedeli prendano di nuovo parte più attiva*) in church worship services. Some months after the publication, the Pope added an important deed to his word as spoken in the Motu-Proprio by commissioning an official publication of Gregorian music.[22] As far as music was concerned, the primary result of this would be the *Graduale Romanum* (1908) of the Editio Vaticana, prepared by the monks of Solesmes, and still in use today.

A quarter of a century later Pope Pius XI, in the apostolic constitution *Divini cultus*,[23] saw himself forced to regret that in some places the wise instruction of Pius X was still not sufficiently complied with, and that therefore the desired fruit had not been harvested. In any case, that was also true for the Netherlands (see §4.2.). The constitution *Divini cultus* was of importance for the Netherlands, however, chiefly because of its plea for establishing boys' choirs and because of its entirely new articulation (*Divini cultus* XI) of the active participation of the people, who must not attend the liturgical rite as strangers or spectators, but also must sing themselves, alternating with the choir. In the Netherlands *Divini cultus* would be a new weapon in the hands of those striving to improve liturgical practice. These were not first and foremost the leaders of the NSGV, but chiefly religious congregations that performed mission work within the Netherlands in what was called *Miswekenwerk*.[24] This programme gave an important role to encouraging the people's participation in the liturgy through their joining in the singing of acclamations and the Gregorian ordinarium, and the implementation of a gymnastic system of liturgical kneeling, sitting and standing.

[22] *Motu-Proprio sull'edizione Vaticana dei libri liturgici, contenenti le melodie gregoriane* d.d. 25 April 1904 (Leiden 1904).

[23] *Apostolische Constitutie over de gestadige bevordering van de liturgie en den gregoriaanschen* zang d.d. 20 December 1928 (Utrecht 1929).

[24] See for instance P. AL & M. SCHNEIDERS (eds.): *Een soort onschuldige hobby* (Heeswijk 1992).

4.2. Catholic Netherlands

The historian Jan Roes (b. 1939) describes the developments in Dutch Catholicism after 1890 as a social movement, a mobilisation of people and resources to change existing social, political and cultural attitudes, both to acquire an equal position in society, and for Catholics to maintain and strengthen a place recognisably their own in respect to other groups in society.[25] Particularly in the years around the turn of the century, Catholic revitalisation received a powerful stimulus as a result of new aesthetic ideals being expressed by Catholic poets and musicians. Their ideal could no longer be the trumpeting of the earlier swaggering *ecclesia militans*, however many understandable reasons there were for it, and instead became a subjective/experienced devotion that is the *unio mystica* of truth and beauty.[26] For them the older church music became an objectionable clamour. The composer of this period who has remained best known is Alphons Diepenbrock (1862-1921), whose 1895 *Missa duobus choris vocum virorum cum organi concentu cantanda* became the grounds for discussion of many antithetical positions regarding musical aesthetics.

A new self-confidence and urge for renewal was also coming to the fore in other ecclesiastical art. Progressive young people in particular not only fought battles against Catholic isolation and clericalism, but also exercised their right to openly criticise aspects of Catholic life. They were no longer willing to dissemble about the cultural backwardness, and wanted an end to conformity and smugness.

In 1925 a survey of Catholic youth showed that the open critique of two decades before had developed into a new direction. Values for which people in the past had fought so fiercely no longer seemed to call up the expected response. Especially organisational life, once an indication of a dawning sense of community, appeared to no longer answer any felt needs. The youth were dynamic, and spontaneously changed their organisations into youth movements. Jazz became popular, and along with cinema, technology interested youth more and more.[27] The new self-consciousness

[25] J. ROES & L. WINKELER: *Tussen Hervorming en vernieuwingen. Een encyclopedisch overzicht van ontwikkelingen in het Nederlands katholicisme sedert de Reformatie, inzonderheid in de 19e en 20e eeuw* (Nijmegen 1994) (= Paper KDC) 75.

[26] ROGIER: *Katholieke herleving* 350.

[27] ROGIER: *Katholieke herleving* 543ff.

described here, and this urge to inward renewal, unfortunately did not run parallel with the tendency for renewal in church music. As it happens, there had been a change in outlook at the NSGV in the meantime.

4.3. The "action" of the NSGV

4.3.1. Acceptance of the Vaticana and papal documents

It took quite a while before the leaders in church music in the Netherlands could work up enthusiasm for the many new things being presented from Rome. Both the question of *parte integrante* from the Motu-Proprio and the restoration of Gregorian song, concretised in the *Editio Vaticana*, gave the gentlemen a good deal to wrestle with. In this regard, the leaders in church music in effect went the way of all flesh: after a period in which they had energetically tried to get the people in the pews to move in new directions, it was asking too much of the earlier pioneers to enthusiastically take the lead once again in the following cultural period. Their reluctance applied to the acceptance of the *Editio Vaticana* for the present. Cecilian and therefore neo-Medicaea minded as they would remain for a long time yet, in its actions the Association would not urgently push to get singing from the *Vaticana* rolling. In fact, the Dutch bishops later felt themselves compelled to request the NSGV in writing to reconcile itself to the new times somewhat more gracefully.[28] Once the *Vaticana* was accepted, the question arose of the rhythmic signs that had been introduced in the Vatican books by the monks of Solesmes as an aid to amateur singers in the performance of Gregorian song. The rhythmic editions once again caused agitation among choir members and the leaders in church music. Now people also had to get used to this. The excuse was that the rhythmic signs were not prescribed by the Pope, only officially tolerated.

4.3.2. NSGV policy

After about 1910 *Tra le sollecitudini* became the basis for the "action" the NSGV undertook to realise those desiderata from the Pope which

[28] Cf. M. HOONDERT: The appropriation of Gregorian plainsong in the Netherlands, 1903-1930, in P. POST, G. ROUWHORST, L. VAN TONGEREN en A. SCHEER (eds.): *Christian feast and festival. The dynamics of Western liturgy and culture* (Leuven 2001) (= Liturgia condenda 12) 655-676.

were mentally achievable for the Association: improving the quality of works of church music, the founding of men's and boys' choirs, the encouragement of the life of choirs by tighter organisation, and the improvement and wider diffusion of Gregorian song. New tasks with regard to the Provincial Synod at Utrecht were specifically the organisation, staffing and maintenance of the censorship committee already instituted at the orders of the bishops in 1904, establishing a professional school for church music, and combatting the fragmentation of activities as a consequence of choirs operating too independently.

Setting up a programme for training professional church musicians took longer in the Netherlands than it did elsewhere. Particularly the costs were an obstacle. There were also few strong leaders among the directors of the NSGV in this period. Furthermore, over the course of time many Dutchmen had gone to study in the schools for church musicians at Regensburg and Aachen. The most important reason for the late start – in 1925 – of the St. Caecilia church music school in Utrecht is that in fact it did not come into existence as a result of *Tra le sollecitudini*,[29] but as a result of the emancipation of Catholics, which in the Netherlands reached its high point precisely in the 1920s. The Motu-Proprio did lead to the diligent organisation of courses for singers, directors and organists in many places. The Association could also count among its activities the distribution of printed educational and informational materials, giving model performances during Gregorian days, setting up a library, and making a contribution to music education both in Catholic primary and secondary schools, and through the Catholic Radio Network. Even in the flowering of the efforts to organise Catholic life, when it had been carried to its furthest, not everything was successful. For instance, there were few results to show for the three-day events organised for clerical singers and retreats for singers which the NSGV also promoted.

The censorship committee advocated by the Motu-Proprio especially appeared to be an effective means of promoting the ideals of the NSGV. As its task, this committee was given all new musical works which were offered for use during the liturgy, to pass judgement on them, and give or deny them the Nihil Obstat, thereby approving them for, or barring them from use in churches. According to Article 7 of the bylaws, the

[29] Most of the professional schools for church music in Europe were, as we have noted, founded before the appearance of *Tra le sollecitudini*.

censors were to base their judgement specifically on the principles and prescriptions of the Motu-Proprio of 1903. Thus they must carefully consider the correctness and completeness of the text, and the question of whether the composition sufficiently fulfilled the demands regarding sanctity, artistic value and universality. Those compositions already existing and in use which no longer met these strictly applied criteria were rigorously struck from the list by diocesan censorship boards. Many choirs experienced this action as a sort of inquisition. In any case, the operation did not take place without resistance, or without considerable regret at the loss of so much beauty. Many choirs, to their sorrow, saw more than half of their cherished repertoire scrapped, and sometimes as much as 90%. In the correspondence[30] between the choirs and the censorship committee, various times there are references to the "hell" which was set up in some choir lofts, to which all the damned materials were relegated. In view of some pleas to still, please, permit a rejected mass to be sung, for instance until the following year at the pastor's jubilee, it would appear the hatchet method, helped by the spirit of the times, had at least partial effect on obedient choirs. The commission, whose ranks, particularly in later years, were not always filled with persons of competence, time and again appears to have employed the standards of "sanctity" and "true art" from the Motu-Proprio of Pius X rather conservatively – clearly following their instincts. Until into the 1950s they would also have problems with the use of chromatic and modern sounds from the post-Cecilian period.

4.4. A singing people

As *Tra le sollecitudini* had confirmed existing practice and provided it with a general ecclesiastical seal of approval, so the constitution *Divini cultus* joined the argument for more active participation by the people in the singing with a general social interest in Dutch folk songs. That these latter received more attention before the Mass and after the Benediction, especially in the musical practice of the confraternities and processions which were revitalised in the second half of the nineteenth century, was in part a consequence of the renaissance in folk music in Western Europe. In the first quarter of the twentieth century a rising branch of scholarship, musicology, devoted considerable attention to the nature and

[30] See the Enquête (survey) held by the Archdiocese in the years 1905-1906.

quality of song in its many forms. In particular, the glorious flowering of old Dutch song became an object for study.[31] For a time folk song underwent a revival, and all was done to stimulate and improve this part of the national heritage. The people must be encouraged in every possible way to sing again.[32] Folk songs were viewed as a real folk art, practised on the streets, at work and in domestic life. It was characteristic of the spirit of the times that in church practice, the art of this genre was found to lie chiefly in the melodies, text and rhythm, and less in the performance and with the performers, while the latter in fact determined the former. Supported by the Motu-Proprio, people also applied the characteristics of the art of the folk song, sung by a single person or a small group, and therefore with a character entirely of its own, to the devotional church song, sung by a larger group. Thus, in the judgement of 'connoisseurs', this latter genre generally came off rather poorly.

As a defender of Gregorian song and polyphony, the NSGV was strongly against the rising practice of folk song around, or during, the celebration of the liturgy. The latter was, of course, strictly forbidden by the ecclesiastical authorities – but this was a ban which, in view of the prevailing spirit of the times, was constantly being flouted. Furthermore, in the spirit of the times, they wrestled with the nature and spirit of devotional songs themselves. The conflict centred around a presumed difference in nature between the devotional songs in church, and folk songs sung outside church. Was a devotional song an expression of art, thus of a single author, or just the opposite, the musical form of the untrained, of the masses, though perhaps sung by an individual? According to some, justice could only be done to it in the mouths of a mass of untrained individuals, who gave form to their collectivity in the singing; others wanted more to hear it from the mouth of a single performer, who had an understanding of what they were doing, as an expression of art. After the publication of *Divini cultus*, a resolution was inevitable: giving a voice to the people essentially implied an attack on the nineteenth century vision of the artistic calibre of the folk song. The

[31] Cf. for example F. VAN DUYSE: *Het oude Nederlandsche lied* (Den Haag/Antwerpen 1903); J. KNUTTEL: *Het geestelijk lied in de Nederlanden vóór de kerkhervorming* (Rotterdam 1906); H.F. WIRTH: *Der Untergang des Niederländischen Volksliedes* (Den Haag 1911).

[32] In 1910 a Roman Catholic association for folk song was established in Den Bosch, and in 1911 the diocese of Haarlem and the archdiocese of Utrecht followed.

world of church music was challenged for the first time to grant a song, sung by an unpractised community, a unique artistic value of its own. It was a difficult struggle, which would flare up again and again, most heavily later with the acknowledgement of the vernacular as a liturgical language by the Second Vatican Council.

4.5. Opposition to Cecilianism

Over the long run, it was inevitable that some church musicians began to have increasing problems with the rigid (and so German) Cecilian straitjacket that was tailored for them by clerical church music leaders. The nineteenth century criteria for the "sound" of church music were, to the minds of these church musicians, more capable of being combined with modern rhythms and harmonies than the gentlemen of the NSGV thought. Collisions between church musicians and particularly the censorship committee and its inflexible measuring stick could therefore not be avoided. In fact, the confrontation was between the nineteenth century on the one side, with its ideas about the effect of musical sounds, defined by Romanticism, and on the other side the twentieth century, with its new views about what music does to and for people, and what the suitable sounds for that are. At the same time, of course, the Liturgical Movement, as it moved forward, also played a role. Functionalism, objectivity and especially the growth of active participation by "the people" *in actu* were of increasingly greater importance.

A whole new sound began to be heard in the generation around the composer Hendrik Andriessen (1892-1981), whose Sacred Heart Mass (1919) had a visionary "people's" character. He, and several of his followers such as Albert de Klerk (1917-1998) and Herman Strategier (1912-1988) gained reputations which transcended the borders of the Netherlands.[33] More and more the work of the new generation diverged from the nineteenth century sense of personal piety: no effects for the sake of effect, no more self-caused manifestation of personal

[33] T.J. DOX: *Hendrik Andriessen, his life and works* (Rochester 1969); T. VAN ECK: Hendrik Andriessen (1892-1981) zum 100. Geburtstag, in *Ars organi* 60 (1992) 78-87; M.D. SCHELL: *A performers' Guide to representative organ works of Hendrik Andriessen* (Ann Arbor/Michigan 1995). See about Andriessen, De Klerk and Strategier also *Die Musik in Geschichte und Gegenwart* I (1999) 685-590 and *The New grove Dictionary of Music and Musicians* I (1995) 414-417; about De Klerk *The New Grove* X (1995) 108; about Strategier *The New Grove* XVIII (1995) 201-202.

feelings, no church music as pure, autonomous art. Andriessen's music is objective, often conceived in broad outlines, entirely in keeping with the new church architecture of his day, among which the works of the architect A.J. Kropholler (1882-1973) can be mentioned. Andriessen's generation moved the accent in church music away from the concertante choir and shifted it to the churchgoer as auditor. They laid the foundation for liturgical practice in which the new ideas regarding liturgy and the actively listening and celebrating community would help to determine the musical form of the celebration. The *Missa Christus Rex* (1938) for double choirs by Andriessen himself, and the *Missa Cathedralis* (1960) by Herman Strategier are striking examples of this new style. In this new style, the *Et incarnatus est* from the Credo from the *Missa in honorem beatae Mariae virginis*, by the then up-and-coming composer Bernard Huijbers, S.J., was not the traditional still genuflection reminiscent of the manger scene or the Consecration, but the loudly-sung high point of the whole composition. Naturally, for the most part ordinary parish choirs had little to do with this *bon ton*, generally because of the rather difficult nature of the compositions. They stuck with the Cecilian masses and motets by, particularly, Lorenzo Perosi and the German Cecilians, which had been spreading further since the 1920s.

The leaders in church music continued to shudder at the thought of an autonomous development in church music, a reaction which can easily be understood in terms of the battle carried out against the old nineteenth century concert practices. Even later in the twentieth century modern music never really reached the liturgy. A part of the reason was that the possibilities for an entirely new sacred music that arose in a post-Andriessen phase found no acceptance in the Church. Among the causes for this were the Church's general recoil from the language of Euterpe, which always strives for a certain autonomy, and, not the least of the causes, continuing hidebound Dutch policies regarding church music, in which the gaze remained fixed on the past. Also, as ever, the taste of the churchgoers, which naturally was focused on familiar music, played a large role in liturgical policy. Finally, clerical domination of the practice of church music, which we have already mentioned and which would continue for too long, had its influence. Progressive clergy have always been exceptions in the history of church music.

5. After the Second World War

5.1. Introduction

The sociologists Goddijn and Van Tillo and the historian Jacobs entitled their book on Catholics in the Netherlands from 1945 to 2000 *Tot vrijheid geroepen*[34] (Called to freedom), thereby making a direct link with the standard work by Rogier on Dutch Catholics in the preceding hundred years, which we have already cited. In choosing this title, the authors have intended to draw a parallel with the past. According to them, since 1945 Dutch Catholics have once again undergone a regeneration and acquired a new spiritual freedom, now, after a period of five years of the Second World War – not so much as a socially relevant segment of the population, but as participants in a process of spiritual renewal, in which the Roman Catholic segment of the population felt itself called to assume a new identity for itself. The new publication describes this development as a natural growth process, which necessarily ran in an oscillating movement: after a period of tension between the urge toward restoration and the urge to renewal (1945-1960), the latter appeared to gain the upper hand, leading to a decade of experimentation (1960-1970). Regression followed in the years between 1970 and 1985; these were years of diversity and fragmentation, in which the struggle for direction led to politicisation and polarisation. In a certain sense it was after this – after 1985 – that renewal again had its turn: a search for new engagement, for the value of the Christian inheritance at the end of the twentieth century.

To a great extent, liturgical music also developed along this line during the period 1945-2000. When the thread of free church life was again picked up after the Second World War, the tension between old and new revealed itself in a newly revived antithesis between the two views regarding the function of music in liturgy which by now had become classic: as an expression of applied art by a trained choir, or, on the contrary, an expression of the untrained, singing community. The later universally lauded "happy sixties" were years that both saw the revitalisation of authentic Roman liturgical forms, and the exploration of the possibilities for bringing one's unique culture into liturgy. For a long

[34] W. Goddijn, J. Jacobs, G. van Tillo: *Tot vrijheid geroepen. Katholieken in Nederland: 1946-2000* (Baarn 1999).

time, this was termed the period of acculturation. In contrast to the general description of those years mentioned in the previous paragraph, from a liturgical-musical perspective the period 1970-1985 can in retrospect be evaluated as thoroughly positive. The "diversity and fragmentation", as it happens, produced at the same time a pluriformity of liturgical expression and a continued urge toward experimentation, particularly in certain influential spawning grounds for new ideas such as the Amsterdam Study Group for Vernacular Liturgy.[35] In addition to being very complex, it was at the same time highly productive for the further inculturation of liturgy. Moreover, in hindsight it appears to have been the beginning of another period of revitalisation, one which was no longer based only on renewal of traditional musical genres, but on the inculturation of characteristic autochthonous forms of expression in musical language. This development became more manifest especially after 1985: secularisation, which had brought an end to the concept of the mass church, appears to have launched reflection regarding what has been termed distinct sacrality and the unique language of liturgical music. Increasingly the values of music in social life appeared to contribute to the wealth of possibilities for musical expression in liturgy, celebrated through a pluriform church, composed of individuals attending voluntarily.

5.2. Church and society

After the end of the Second World War the call for renewal in society and politics was sounded in all quarters. Although the desired breakthrough failed to materialise, and many yearned for the restoration of old values, the Catholic segment of the population as a whole would also begin to stir. The war had taught people to think critically and stand up for themselves. Particularly the openness toward those who thought differently which had grown during the war quietly continued to gain ground. There were also increasing signals from within the Church that it no longer was standing with both feet in the reality of modern society. The bishops, who held that openness was only safe

[35] According to many, in these years the Amsterdam Study Group was no longer part of the Roman Catholic Church – or at least not of the traditional Roman Catholic Church.

from a position of strong Catholic unity,[36] did not succeed in calming the unrest in spiritual care.[37] After 1955 the movement for renewal in the Dutch Catholic Church increased sharply, and the "hour of the layman" began to dawn. In 1958 Rogier proposed that among sheep, submissiveness to the shepherd is not a virtue, but merely a question of instinct.[38] Particularly the 1950s were at the same time years of rapid declericalisation of Catholic society, with the modernisation of Catholic organisations which accompanied this, of rising polarisation, and a feeling of losing one's bearings, chiefly in the areas of church/liturgical life and moral questions. These were the marks of a segment of the population attaining maturity and standing up on its own feet. These were also the years that paved the way to the Second Vatican Council (1961-1965), which neither desired to, nor could, put a stop to these developments.

5.3. Liturgy and church music

Although the practice of what the Church's supporters in the Netherlands called the "rich Roman life" could still be maintained for some years after the war, it appeared that change, which had already presented itself abundantly before the turbid times, would speedily engulf the Church. Of course, various things led to tensions, particularly among the institutions which were active in the field of the Liturgical Movement, such as the *Miswekenwerk* (Mass weeks' work), led primarily by regulars, what was called the *Gemeenschapsmis* (Community Mass), a movement supported more by diocesan clergy, and the NSGV, respectively. All three had their own focus of action, respectively the active participation of the people through dialogues and singing along with the Latin texts, the singing of Dutch songs during a Mass that was not otherwise sung by the celebrant or choir, and finally, the Latin High Mass. The document on which these activities were founded was the papal encyclical *Mediator Dei et hominum*, of November 20, 1947, which was generally considered the *magna carta* of the liturgical movement, as the Motu-Proprio by Pope Pius X had been for church music.

[36] See the episcopal Mandement *De katholiek in het openbare leven van deze tijd* (1954).

[37] ROES & WINKELER: *Tussen Hervorming en vernieuwingen* 19-20.

[38] ROES & WINKELER: *Tussen Hervorming en vernieuwingen* 21.

During these years the policy of the NSGV was directed at the improvement of existing church music rather than innovation. In the *Gregoriusblad*[39] General Chairman J.C. van de Wiel stated that leading choirs back to a pure liturgical spirit was still the first task for the NSGV. He apparently would have gladly added to that, 'preferably in the Cecilian sphere'. For him, choirs continued to have a role as servants in the traditional sense, which particularly as a result of circumstances during the War had become diluted, so that they had slid back in the direction of concert performance and self-glorification, the eternal temptation of every established choir. In his speech celebrating the 70th anniversary of the founding of the Association in 1948, the new General Chairman Dr. A.J.M. Kat (1904-1958) defended the High Mass, sung in its entirety by a choir, as a source of spiritual life in every parish. In his opinion, the task of a choir was first of all spiritual, and the provision of church music a true calling. What was the life of the public worship service still worth, without the splendour of the music? Was the High Mass not the centre of the week for the Church? And was it not the choir who, as it were, delineated the Church year for the people? Perhaps better, and more penetratingly than through many sermons, people learned to understand their faith through empathy with the choir. Seen properly, the choir was the first medium for Catholic Action.[40]

The core of the contrast between the position of the NSGV and liturgists very quickly became the question of the significance of music in liturgy. Particularly in the 1950s, a period when composers were exploring the boundaries of sonority and rhythm, in the music world there was a lot of discussion regarding the relationship of the composer and listener. Articles[41] and letters to the editor asked how far the development of modern music should be allowed to go, and whether the composer's all too personal (and therefore often hermetic) inventions were of any use to society. For the NSGV, church music could not be wholly autonomous. Therefore it could not merely be the free expression of the feelings of the composer. It must serve an end beyond itself, be applied art – but not as understood by the liturgists, as song by and for the community, but rather as people outside the church also wished, as song

[39] J.C.W. VAN DE WIEL: Onze Sint Gregoriusvereniging, in *Gregoriusblad* 67 (1946) 5.
[40] A. KAT: De Hoogmis, in *Gregoriusblad* 69 (1948) 136-137.
[41] Among church musicians, Bernard Huijbers regularly entered the polemic ring.

understood by the community and intended by the composer for the community. For the NSGV, church music remained an expression of art, which could only be accomplished by practitioners who were as skilled as possible. As one might expect, the rediscovery of the song peculiar to liturgy and the community which celebrates liturgy – traditionally called *cantus* ("music to be done") – could not but provoke feelings of irritation and opposition from choirs, who simply conceived music chiefly as *musica* (music to be listened to), as adornment for sacred action. Many leaders of the NSGV continued to prefer viewing active participation, as it was expressed in the encyclical *Mediator Dei*, in the sense of Pius X (true art/sanctity) and only barely in the spirit of *Divini cultus* (1928), which, for the rest, choirs accommodated as much as possible in its formulation of the active participation of the people.

Yet they did go a step further. Without having to give up the supposed autonomy of its choirs, in the following period the NSGV could indeed take a positive stance regarding modern church music, and thus acknowledge the Cecilian sound of earlier times as passé. Because this meant the end of the all-male choir, the NSGV devoted itself to the establishment of boys' choirs, which indeed were formed in large numbers, right down to in the smallest parishes. For the best choirs the ideal church music was now the somewhat older Mass of Alphons Diepenbrock, and for the better choirs the works of the generation of composers around Hendrik Andriessen, already mentioned. These young composers felt themselves inspired by *Mediator Dei* and the example of Andriessen to reorient the traditional components of the polyphonic ordinarium to their liturgical function. In doing this, they attempted to avoid sentimentality, bravura and baroque expression of the text as much as possible. In retrospect it appears that they also were one of the bridges between the old Latin liturgical music and the community liturgy in the vernacular which was to come. This is found particularly in many of their compositions from the 1950s, which on the one hand, to be sure, were characterised by the traditional motet style, but on the other hand bore traces of a search for new word-sound relationships in which the direct expression of the text becomes prominent. It goes without saying that this latter brought them to the use of the Dutch language. Because their compositions in this style were therefore unsuitable for the liturgy that was still in Latin, they were sung as 'encores' after the end of a High Mass or vespers, primarily as psalm settings with an extensive antiphon.

Even more significant than these developments in the preparation for the community liturgies to come were the activities of the *Misweken-werk* and the *Gemeenschapsmis* movement, mentioned above. The former consisted primarily of a sort of practice-oriented parish retreat, the goal of which was to bring the people closer to the liturgy. Thanks to these homeland mission activities, a number of forms and degrees of participation in the liturgy through dialogues and singing along with the Gregorian ordinarium by the people became fashionable, which were copied from the German *Bet-singmesse*, *Gemeinschaftsmesse* and *Deutsches Hochambt*, among others. The activities of the *Gemeen-schapsmis*, which had in view the singing of Dutch language songs during a read Mass on Sunday, were based on the encyclical *Musicae sacrae disciplina* (1955), which had among its recommendations the singing of songs in the vernacular. This singing of songs in the vernacular during a spoken Mass had already been a practice in the Netherlands from around the beginning of the twentieth century during weekday children's Masses. Particularly through the work of the Amsterdam pastor Jacob Duijves new liturgical-devotional strophic songs appeared, which were published in *Gemeenschapsmis*, the first Dutch collection with new liturgical songs.[42]

6. Around the Second Vatican Council

6.1. Church life

The 1960s were a decade of great change in various areas of church life in the Netherlands, as they were also everywhere else. In part as a consequence of Pope John XXIII's call for *aggiornamento*, bringing the church up to date with the times, a passionate movement for pastoral renewal got under way at the beginning of the 1960s. Among its consequences were that the Church went from being "Roman" to being "Dutch". Many things which until then had been considered by believers as fundamental for their religious life disappeared, fell into disuse or were transformed: the Holy Mass changed its face and became a celebration of the Eucharist, or just "worship"; individual confession fell into disuse and was replaced by public repentance; the regulations

[42] *Gemeenschapsmis* (Hilversum 1958).

regarding fasting and abstinence were abolished; home visits by the pastor or curate and devotional practices (Lauds, Congregations, Third Orders, the rosary, processions, retreats) fell into disuse. The priesthood descended into a crisis which expressed itself chiefly around the question of celibacy,[43] in the drastic decline in vocations for the priesthood, and in the concentration of theological training institutes. Between 1967 and 1972 the number of Roman Catholic clergy in the Netherlands decreased by almost 4000. With declericalisation came democracy: laity too wanted to, and could be responsible for evangelisation and church life. The new understanding of the Church reached its climax in the Pastoral Council of the Dutch Archdiocese, which was held in Noordwijkerhout between 1966 and 1970, and that brought the then rather progressive Dutch bishops into conflict with Rome. The quick changes in church life, and the often shocking way they occurred, could ultimately not take place without tensions. The about-face from a vertical to an horizontally experienced faith gave many vertigo and left them discontented. Many in the Church suffered, not the least among them conservative church musicians.

6.2. Liturgy

Perhaps there was no area in the Roman Catholic Church – with the possible exception of habits of the religious – where the movement for renewal was so visible as in the changes in the field of liturgy. Indeed, "facing the people" was nowhere more visible, and thus more noted by the ordinary churchgoer, than through the turning around of the altar in the first half of the 1960s. This sometimes drastic simplification and the rebuilding of church interiors which accompanied it was experienced by some as a second "breaking of the images". Perhaps 1964 was the key year: the Dutch bishops devoted their annual Lenten pastoral letter to the rediscovery and renewal of the liturgy, and in October of that year they announced various innovations for the Dutch dioceses such as the official introduction of the vernacular (with the exception of the eucharistic prayer), which was to begin the first Sunday of Advent.

[43] In the Netherlands, from 1960 to 1970 1037 priests (seculars and regulars) would leave the priesthood. The high water mark was 1969, with 244 resignations.

The episcopal guidelines threw the world of church music further into thorough agitation. For the time being, the Latin texts were translated into Dutch.[44] It is to the credit of the Amsterdam Study Group for Vernacular Liturgy, established in 1961 (thus before Vatican II), that they took the lead in the process of growing toward a liturgy celebrated "by chancel and congregation alike", as the title of a publication by the most important composer of the day, Bernard Huijbers, expressed it.[45] Especially the poet Huub Oosterhuis very quickly began to argue for employing what was called the "second language", which, to put it briefly, was not that of the tractate but that of the Muses.[46] Many texts were created in local circles, and did not always rise above the level of moralism and dilettantism. Local and regional liturgical centres, assisted by a photocopier, three-ring notebooks and spiral binders, provided for the wide distribution of these self-made products. The unstable and experimental character of all this was typical of the 1960s. The appearance of the new altar missal *Ordo Missae* in 1969, a Dutch translation of which was published in 1970 as the *Missaal*, did finally provide some direction.

In addition to the variety of texts used, liturgical practice was characterised by subjectivism and pluriformity. Liturgies were no longer handed down from above, but were generally conceived by local liturgical study groups that generally operated with support of a particular group, often all of the same age bracket. Opponents spoke somewhat denigratingly of "consumer liturgy". The liturgies on offer concentrated around youth masses, family masses (often in fact children's masses), thematic services, Latin High Masses and services for house churches. By a rough estimate in 1970 there were about 1100 liturgical study groups in the Netherlands, with about 10,000 members, of which 734 were parochial study groups in 1428 parishes. The earlier Sunday church attendance, which had been assumed as a matter of course for Catholics, declined drastically in the 1960s, and for many the decision on whether they would attend a service or not depended on the liturgy being offered that weekend. The fading of religious practice made church attendance fall back from 64.6% in 1966 to 46.3% in 1970.

[44] Later this was called the phase of acculturation.

[45] B. HUIJBERS: *Door podium en zaal tegelijk. Volkstaalliturgie en muzikale stijl. Vijf en een half essay over muzikale functionaliteit* (Hilversum 1969 / Baarn 1994).

[46] H. OOSTERHUIS: De tweede taal, in *In het voorbijgaan* (Utrecht 1968) 236-244.

This downward trend did not cease with the beginning of the 1970s: in 1991 weekly attendance at mass has fallen to 13.1%.[47]

6.3. Church music

6.3.1. Tension between tradition and innovation

The new word-sound relationship as a consequence of the new functionality of music in liturgy lay at the root of the revolutionary developments in the 1960s in the field of church music. The community must be given a voice basically by being involved as a singing church, next to and together with the singing choir. From now on it would be a matter of song essentially coming from the community, putting it in motion and bringing it to a tighter unity. It was no longer a question of edification, and not glorification above all else, but, functionally, of everyone singing together. In the first years that chiefly meant a simplification of melodies, emphasis on singing in unison – and in the eyes of the traditionalists, an enormous amateurism in the singing. All these things resulted in a grand church music culture coming to a rather abrupt end.

Understandably, the new vision of liturgical music led to division in the liturgical-musical world. On the one side there were the established (and largely male) choirs,[48] who still took refuge in their traditional bastion, the Latin High Mass. They were supported by the NSGV, and felt themselves no less validated by the pronouncements of the Council, which were capable of being interpreted in more than one way, and by the evangelical efforts of the *Miswekenwerk*, which was approaching its end. On the other side there were the still young mixed choirs of the "new" liturgy, all children of the *Gemeenschapsmis* movement. A painful consequence of the new developments was the embitterment of perhaps most of the traditional church musicians. They experienced the new word-sound relationship as a movement in which the ground for their existence was being swept away. A church musician devoted to the liturgy like Herman Strategier went through a serious mental crisis in the 1960s that he – and alas that was not the case with so many of his

[47] Cf. T. SCHEPENS: De Nederlandse katholieken en hun kerk: een statistische documentatie, in GODDIJN, JACOBS & VAN TILLO: *Tot vrijheid geroepen* 499-525.

[48] Boys' choirs had already disappeared in most places around 1960.

colleagues – only overcame in the mid-1970s, thanks to considerable and intense conversations with the pastor of his then parish.

6.3.2. Continuation of the traditional motet style

In the period in which the traditional forms and genres were merely given a new lease on life by translating the Latin into Dutch, many composers did not have to feel they were sidetracked, because the old views with regard to the word-sound relationship were not yet essentially eroded. Among church composers many felt drawn by the idea (and by the NSGV) to begin to set the newly translated texts of the earlier Latin ordinarium and proprium in the traditional forms and in the traditional style, termed the motet style, in which, as in the classical motet, considerable attention and expressiveness went into the independent melody and its polyphonic fabric of voices. Although sometimes of outstanding quality, the motet genre could not go on. It had no future, and would soon be left behind by the new relation between word and sound, or practically speaking, by the new liturgical song, new in language and melody – particularly by those of the Amsterdam Study Group for Vernacular Liturgy. When, toward the end of the 1960s liturgical practice became more and more characterised by the "song culture" so detested by the traditionalists, the NSGV could no longer hang back, and wore itself out organising amateur courses everywhere in the country, chiefly for directors and organists. This change of attitude could take place within the Association in part thanks to the vision of new Directors, who were able to read the signs of the times. For the rest, in the pluriform liturgical offerings, Gregorian song and the motet style would continue to have their place.

6.3.3. Community liturgy

Within several years the Dutch Roman Catholic Church in the 1960s became a singing church. In this decade, in which the whole of society changed shape, the formation of community liturgy also fundamentally took place. Songs based on the old devotional songs were now replaced by new liturgical songs, among which especially those by the poet Huub Oosterhuis and the composer Bernard Huijbers would become enormously popular. A close second were the new body of songs from the Reformation churches. Indeed, particularly their new rhymed version of the psalms from 1967, and the new repertoire of hymns which accompanied it,[49] had great influence on Roman Catholic liturgy. An important new characteristic of the community liturgy was the participation of the people through other genres than that of the strophic song, such as acclamation, responses and antiphons. As well as the new songs, the Amsterdam Study Group pointed the way with the revitalisation of various forms of psalmody (antiphonal singing), primary expressions of community singing. Finally, it was typical of this chaotic but nevertheless fruitful period that policy in the liturgical-musical field was to a large extent determined by the publishers of liturgical music. A very original spirituality was heard from the extensive *Abdijboek*, a completely Dutch sung breviary for contemplative monastic communities, which was published after 1967, and was assembled by the Intermonastery Study Group for Liturgy, a collaboration of Benedictine and Cistercian monks and nuns.

In addition to the Amsterdam Study Group, a decisive impetus for inculturation was in no less degree given to church music by the youth services which sprang from the ground everywhere in the country. These were prepared, and the music provided, by choirs large and small, and combos, introducing texts, melodies and rhythms of various calibers. Through these, American Negro spirituals, British beat music and pop music entered the church. In the years discussed here, music of this sort was in general more serviceable for the choir itself and for the listening public than it was for the community liturgy. The youth choirs established the tradition for liturgy celebrations for, and provided by, special groups. These drew an audience of their own, and in many respects continued the old practice of the traditional choirs with their grand polyphonic Latin Masses, for these too were autonomous events which attracted many who wished to just let the music pour over them, down below in the church. At the beginning of the 1970s the Dutch Roman Catholic Church had a total of almost 5000 choirs, with 134,000 members, 4000 of which, with a total of 96,000 members, were associated with parishes. Both as a consequence of the exodus from the church and the new views regarding the nature of community liturgy, membership in one of the many study groups, with which every parish was blessed, was the entrée for participation in the liturgy. Among these study groups, the choirs occupied the most important place.

[49] Cf. *Liedboek voor de Kerken* (Den Haag 1973).

7. Bernard Huijbers and the Amsterdam Study Group for Vernacular Liturgy

7.1. Biography

A separate paragraph on Bernard Huijbers is desirable. In the tumultuous 1960s and '70s, there was no one who so defined the development of liturgy in the Netherlands, in word and music, as he did. Bernard Maria Huijbers was born in Rotterdam, July 2, 1922. His parents' subsequent move to Amsterdam in 1928 shaped his life decisively, as because of this he came to be registered as a pupil at the Jesuit Ignatius College there in 1934. He remained there after his student years, first as a "scholasticus" of the Society, which he entered in 1940, and later as the song leader at chapel and outside it, and as a teacher of school music. In 1954 he was ordained priest. In the meantime he had studied music theory and school music at the Amsterdam Conservatory, and taken private lessons on the viola. In 1963 he became a lecturer in liturgy at the Amsterdam Conservatory. He taught this same subject from 1969 to 1978 at the Dutch Institute for Church Music in Utrecht. In 1970 he withdrew as an instructor in school music, and resigned from the Society of Jesus. In 1978 he also left Amsterdam physically, moving to France. Some time passed before he began to compose again. Isolated from their earlier roots, his later works are characterised by a wholly different word-sound relationship than his previous work. If the power of his "Amsterdam" works lay in their expressivity, multiple layers of meaning and zest, those from the French period are more romantic and imposing in nature. Their style is more or less neo-Brahms.

7.2. Strophic songs

Huijbers's adventures in Dutch language liturgy began in 1959 with a setting of the Passion of St. John. Together with Huub Oosterhuis, his colleague at Ignatius College, with whom he would work closely after 1960, he was in search for alternatives for the traditional devotional celebrations in the chapel of the boys school. For the present, the Sunday liturgy was untouchable, not only because this was still reserved for the Latin liturgy, but also because it was the practice for pupils to go home to their parents for the weekends. Out of this search came the *Adventsliturgie* for Advent, 1960, and the *Vastenliturgie* (Lenten liturgy) and

Pinksterliturgie (Pentecost liturgy) in 1961. Huijbers called these first products "framing songs", strophic songs that "framed" the liturgy. Actually, his talents were not called upon so much during this period, as Huub Oosterhuis wrote his texts to be set to familiar tunes. What was new in these first songs was that from the very start they radically threw off their devotional yoke: their text was liturgical, and their melody that of the old, expressive Dutch folk song. In a second phase Huijbers began to write new melodies for the text contrafracts by Oosterhuis. Inspired by these new melodies, Oosterhuis in turn wrote new texts for the new melodies by Huijbers. That is how, for example, the song *Wat altijd is geweest* (What has always been) came to be: first Oosterhuis wrote his text as a contrafract for a melody from the Genevan Psalter, and subsequently Huijbers wrote a new melody for the text. Huijbers and Oosterhuis only definitively found each other as collaborators when the latter stopped writing texts for folk songs, and presented new texts directly to Huijbers to be set to music. That was the period in which the gospel and communion songs were created, which were later almost all to become a part of the body of Dutch liturgical songs, and are still being sung to this day. As a liturgist, in this period (around 1960) Oosterhuis also opted for revitalising traditional liturgical genres, from which the first acclamations and recitatives arose.

7.3. Psalmody

An important subsequent phase in the life of the Amsterdam liturgical renewal movement was initiated in 1961 with the establishment of the Student Study Group for Vernacular Liturgy, followed in 1962 by the Amsterdam Study Group for Vernacular Liturgy which became so familiar, set up by its initiator Jan van Kilsdonk, along with others. Attention now focused chiefly on psalmody, the preparation of Dutch psalms in the responsive or antiphonal genre. Huijbers has always explained that he learned how to work with psalms from his fellow Jesuit, Joseph Gelineau. Huijbers viewed Gelineau's book *Chant et musique dans le culte chrétien*[50] as a pioneering work in community liturgy. Toward the end of the 1950s "psalms by Gelineau" were being sung everywhere in the Netherlands. After 1964 they were succeeded by Huijbers's own settings, which were directly conceived for the Dutch language: *Drie*

[50] J. GELINEAU: *Chant et musique dans le culte chrétien* (Paris 1962).

Beurtzangen from Psalm 25 (1964) and *Negen Beurtzangen* (1966). These are redolent of the atmosphere of the international study group *Universa Laus*, founded in Lugano, Switzerland, in 1966, where Huijbers and Gelineau met once again. Gelineau worked for the restoration of the old responsive and antiphonal psalmody, sung by a leader and community in non-strophic form. In his book *Door podium en zaal tegelijk*,[51] Huijbers frequently uses the term "elementary music", borrowed from Carl Orf. For Huijbers elementary music is music that has enough elementary turns to give a melody both variety and excitement. The musical elements he is referring to are, as it were, the building blocks of melody. As Huijbers explains,

> I began to compose differently as a result of the encyclical *Mediator Dei*, which had in mind reorientating the musical Mass to the liturgy. I began to consciously ask myself what is going on in the parts of the ordinarium, what their place and structure was. In that, I was following in the footsteps of Hendrik Andriessen(...) After the war, it was beginning to make itself felt here and there(...) Around 1950 I was still a proponent of introducing classes in church Latin in the schools, because the people had to learn to understand Latin. That's what the Liturgical Movement wanted too, and Jungmann, with his *Missarum Sollemnia*!(...) Later I realised that something like that was utopian. It is not only impossible to teach the people Latin, but it must be more immediate(...) Thus I became a proponent of the *Gemeenschapsmis*, with its Dutch strophic songs. Gelineau's view that the Psalms were *the* songs for the Mass was a new step. While in the Netherlands we thought that something like that could only work through rhymed psalms, Gelineau was able to make the translations of the psalms in the Jerusalem Bible easily singable in an unrhymed form. Midway through the 1960s we therefore were experimenting already with psalmody, like for instance Psalm 25, "Naar U gaat mijn verlangen, Heer"[52](...) Most traditional church musicians of the time lacked a source of inspiration(...) they moved with the liturgists like the two rails of a railway track: together they carry the train, and they go in the same direction, but they never meet(...) Huub Oosterhuis had protested that the bishops required Dutch just like that, because people were not yet ready for participation.
>
> How it happened? In the 1950s in the Ignatius chapel we had a large choir with, for instance, 30 sopranos. For a long time our sung celebration consisted of a *Gemeenschapsmis* with spoken texts from the ordinarium. That

[51] See note 45.

[52] See *Gezangen voor Liturgie* (Baarn 1996^2) 25: 1, 2 and 3.

was not the Sunday Mass. We didn't have one, because the diocese of Haarlem had decided that the students must go to their own parish church on the weekend. We did have a sung Mass from the Maria Congregation once a month on a Sunday. Thus we experimented with other opportunities, such as the 'first Friday' and so forth(...) We had no idea where it was all going to lead. It was a matter of trial and error(...) In 1961 Huub Oosterhuis[53] came to Amsterdam. In 1961 he began to write many new songs(...) We began the Amsterdam Study Group for Vernacular Liturgy in 1962(...)
We got involved in the student ecclesia thanks to Jan van Kilsdonk, who was the moderator there(...) We went outside the Ignatius chapel because without telling me the students, under the leadership of their colleague Nard Loonen, began to promote the new songs and on their own initiative a small group from the choir went to sing in the city jail. I got involved when they asked me to come play the organ one time, when the regular student organist couldn't make it. It was these rascals who brought us – we, who thought we knew everything and could do anything – to the realisation that what we were doing could also be done outside the Ignatius chapel, and that we didn't need a big choir for it. I followed their lead(...) After St. Thomas Church (Christmas, 1965), we began at the Dominicus Church on Low Sunday, 1966. The turning point was Christmas, 1966, when the whole Ignatius community came and celebrated with us. We knew it then: this is where we belonged. As a matter of fact, we couldn't go back, because the Ignatius College chapel couldn't hold all the people who were coming any more.[54]

7.4. The "Dominicus" and new musical genres

More than just the time of great accessibility began on Low Sunday, 1966. The freer situation outside the limiting context of the Jesuit's Ignatius College appeared to be favourable for experiments for the sake of further development of the community liturgy, particularly as Oosterhuis and Huijbers saw this. After a period of revitalisation, in which

[53] Hubertus Gerardus Josephus Henricus Oosterhuis: born November 1, 1933, in Amsterdam; entered the Society of Jesus in 1952; studied Dutch literature at Groningen 1958-1961; ordained priest 1964; resigned from the Society of Jesus 1969. Worked further as a freelance in the Student Ecclesia (after 1970) and De Populier (1972). Oosterhuis's first real liturgical song was "Zolang er mensen zijn op aarde". He wrote it on November 16, 1959, during a bicycle trip from Winsum to Groningen. See K. KOK: *De vleugels van een lied* (Baarn 1990) 21.

[54] Interview with the author of this article, November 18, 1998.

the emphasis lay on the restoration of the original text genres of the Roman liturgy and their musical content, people in the Dominicus community came step by step to the development of new text and melody genres, based on the celebration of liturgy "by chancel and congregation alike". The old Roman liturgy was no longer the fundamental pattern, but more the spiritual framework in which new genres and forms could arise. After a first period of what Huijbers titled "great" pieces, such as the Great Litany of 1967 and the Liturgies for Maundy Thursday, Good Friday and Easter Saturday Night, all from 1968, the first of what came to be called "sung eucharistic prayers" came into being. A eucharistic prayer was sung for the first time on Maundy Thursday. It was a very deliberate choice: it was precisely on that day that people wished to shift the accent from the foot washing to the institution of the Eucharist, and make that prayer the central point of the celebration.

In the meantime, Huijbers's compositions were changing in nature. Their melody and rhythm was becoming freer, more varied, and therefore also less traditional. If for him it had previously been a matter of finding the right form and the right accompanying melodic genre, now it was an issue of contemporary possibilities for the celebrating community. That meant more attention for the language of rhythm, melody and harmony, and freer forms. Huijbers has continually underscored that the basis for all of this did not lie with him as composer, but with the text writer, Huub Oosterhuis. Huijbers was only following upon the changed nature of Oosterhuis's texts. Oosterhuis's freer poetry had consequences for the melody, which now once again took on the character of a song. This development in Huijbers's compositional style indeed comes most clearly to the fore in texts that differ absolutely from traditional liturgical texts, such as *Zwemmen en varen* (Swimming and sailing), or *Niksers, leeghoofden* (Good-for-nothings, bird-brains).

7.5. The 1970s

Around 1975 the day of the Amsterdam Study Group for Vernacular Liturgy has passed. Its consistently progressive products were no longer in keeping with the spirit of the times. The pioneers had gotten so far out front that the followers lost sight of them. The Amsterdam Study Group appeared to have been a child of the "happy sixties". From the middle of the 1970s the "Dutch model" in church music had finished flowering, and the Netherlands again fell into step with the general developments in Western Europe.

Meanwhile, developments in the ecclesiastical field had not left Huijbers unaffected in his personal life. His unorthodox attitude brought him into difficulties with the Jesuits. In 1973 he left the Society. He had in the meantime entered a crisis of faith, and through this had lost a good deal of his compositional power. Not only did he have little initiative to compose, but what he did produce was of notably lesser quality. In 1978 the end came for the Study group for Vernacular Liturgy, and for Huijbers's efforts for Catholic liturgy. He moved to France, where he built a new life – and spiritual life as well – for himself and his life partner.

No one can deny that Huub Oosterhuis and Bernard Huijbers played a unique, important and essential role in the process in which the new liturgy was born and grew up, which in Catholic Netherlands occurred principally between 1960 and 1975. Because the new repertoire of songs for choirs was formed in this period, to this day works by Oosterhuis/Huijbers continue to occupy a prime place in it. Through his very individual attitude, in many respects Huijbers has however remained a loner among his fellow church musicians. The basis of this was a difference in opinion about the artistic worth of music in the church. Until about 1975, for many church musicians this value was still defined by Cecilian and Romantic concepts, while from the very beginning of his experiments with Dutch as a liturgical language, for Huijbers this was defined by the function of a piece within the whole of the celebration. Ultimately it was also about a fundamental judgement about the expressive value of Dutch as a liturgical language.

8. Stabilisation, renewal and widening

Midway through the 1970s the period of experimentation was almost over, and it appeared that the forms of liturgical music were beginning to stabilise. As a consequence of further secularisation of church life, and habituation leading to new, established rituals, it became less noisy in the liturgical-musical camp, and a sort of status quo set in. The ancient qualities of any liturgical action, such as rituality and thus also identifiability and repetition, once again took hold. The worth of a liturgical song was in part determined by this. A song no longer needed to be newly made to be able to speak to people. All this was also in part a consequence of a spirit of restoration that wafted through liturgy. Positive sides of old concepts such as "sentiment" and "devotion" were rediscovered. Where people in many parishes had for some years sung the Oosterhuis/Huijbers *Heden zult gij zijn glorie aanschouwen* (Today you shall see His glory) as the processional at the beginning of a Christmas Eve Mass, this song was now traded in, not for a Gregorian Introitus, but for a Dutch version of *O Come, All Ye Faithful.* The expressive musical language of the recent past was supplemented, and often replaced, by a more romantic and imposing word-sound relation. The works by Antoine Oomen (b. 1945), such as for instance his *Licht dat ons aanstoot in de morgen* (Light that strikes us in the morning), are for the most part written in this spirit. The hot topics in professional church music journals in these years were the place and function of multiple parish choirs that often operated independently, the content of the position of church musician, and the related question of the relation between functionality and art. Specifically, among the topics concerned were Gregorian song, the traditional Latin repertoire, and the legitimacy of non-traditional texts, harmonies and rhythms.

8.1. New movements in church music

Many viewed the new era as a time of catching up after the in many respects one-sided course of development in the 1960s. Music was now heard in the church which had never been entirely silenced, but through the success of Huijbers had been relegated to the background. Composers who for a long time had imagined themselves to be written off, such as Albert de Klerk and Herman Strategier, could experience a new creative period. The sounds of others such as Maurice Pirenne (b. 1928), who had never fallen silent, now were heard all the more clearly. An understandable development too was that people in many places sought refuge in a repertoire, originally created for an earlier type of liturgy, but in which they found that which was musically necessarily absent in pieces of more recent origin.

Another important development was that slowly a new generation of leaders were taking over the reins in Dutch church music institutions, whose minds were no longer shaped in part by pre-Conciliar ideas, and who had enough zeal to labour *con amore* for community liturgy and for the necessary but slow improvement in quality in liturgy sensitive to inculturation. Policy now took on different aims. If it formerly had to an important degree been about maintaining old forms and values, the focus was now on practical matters, exploring new possibilities and creating space for them. The tensions that this attitude produced every now and then with central ecclesiastical leadership and with the conservative segment of their own followers were in part interpreted positively, namely as a challenge to look at the beaten paths critically. The renewal and widening of the title of this section found its first temporary stabilisation in the general song collection *Gezangen voor Liturgie*. This appeared in 1984, and in its own way marked the new era, as it was the last of an almost countless series of predecessors of all sorts, sizes and content, in which the full wealth of the previous period of experimentation is recorded. *Gezangen voor Liturgie* was the fruit of and response to the stabilisation, and was widely distributed. As such, the collection has had a fundamental influence on shaping the repertoire of choirs in our time, and has become an *editio typica* and point of reference for new publications in the field of liturgical music.

8.2. Ecumenical flowering

Finally, an important development in these years was the height of the flowering of a liturgical movement in the Protestant churches in the Netherlands. The first result of this was the interdenominational *Liedboek voor de Kerken*, presented in 1973. In addition to a new rhymed version of the psalms (1967), it included a selection of strophic songs in which many were new in text and melody, and others derived from the great international *oecumene*. Among the text writers were Willem Barnard (b. 1920), Ad den Besten (b. 1923), Jan Wit (1914-1980), Jan Willem Schulte Nordholt (1920-1995) and Klaas Heeroma (1909-1972). Important composers were Frits Mehrtens (1922-1975), Willem Vogel (b. 1920) and Adriaan Schuurman (1904-1996). The *Liedboek*, the fruit of 'catholic' thought, would also be important for the Roman Catholics. It was one of the factors leading to a more fruitful cooperation with Roman Catholics in all fields of liturgy and church music, such as, for instance, in the area of professional training. The cross-fertilisation and growing consensus became still stronger when in the 1980s the common liturgical foundations of the Christian churches manifested themselves more clearly, thanks both to advancing inculturation and as a consequence of a more high-church liturgy in the

Protestant churches. A milestone in this process was the publication of the *Dienstboek*, in which considerable space was given to new liturgical forms and genres.[55]

9. AROUND THE YEAR 2000

Toward the end of the twentieth century many were afraid that the development of community liturgy would remain suspended in a hybrid form somewhere between the innovations of the 1960s and the regressive developments of the period which followed. For others this fear was groundless. In their view, it is only in our time that the real community liturgy has been seen. Although distinguishing developments at such a short perspective in time is extremely difficult and uncertain, perhaps there are movements occurring in two directions. On the one hand, proceeding from the Church's liturgical actions themselves, there is continued progress along the path already so long followed, of further inculturation. In this connection, it is relevant that liturgists and musicians continue to find one another in their concern for authentic liturgical acts which no longer just proceed from old forms, but from contemporary human language and actions. Today inculturation is no longer seen as a danger that looms over liturgy, but is experienced as a resource which offers untold possibilities. The ecumenical overtures among the different denominations are also gaining momentum. On the other hand, the questions posed by the many, complex ritual movements in society are becoming clearer. Many studies point to the multiplicity of rituals in human life.[56] It can not be denied that many people feel pain as a result of the supposed deritualisation of social life, and of their unfulfilled search for a place for liturgy in it. Many liturgists and musicians however see in that a reason to try to probe and test this ritual milieu. In this way they search for a point of contact, in order to arrive at the basic anthropological dimensions of liturgy and an understanding of the role of the arts in it.[57]

[55] *Dienstboek. Een proeve. Schrift, Maaltijd, Gebed* (Zoetermeer 1998).

[56] G. LUKKEN: *Rituelen in overvloed* (Baarn 1999); P. POST: Religieuze volkscultuur en liturgie, in J. LAMBERTS: *Volksreligie, liturgie en evangelisatie* (Leuven/Amsersfoort 1998) 19-77.

[57] See the recent publications of P. Post, such as Rituals and the function of the past: rereading Eric Hobsbawm, in *Journal of Ritual Studies* 10 (1998) 85-107.

9.1. Aspects of the culture in the year 2000

What important aspects of contemporary musical culture are of interest for the word-sound discussion? One is perhaps particularly our present-day oral-auditive culture and, as a consequence of it, the familiarity, and thus proverbial contempt, that people have with music from their youngest years. That is very negative. On the other hand, there is a whole new way of relating to music which is anything but inattentive or passive. That is positive.

Since the rise of sound recording, in the Western world music has become ever less an activity and ever more a product. A new auditive tradition has grown up, with far-reaching consequences for the changing way music is received. In the book *Trost für Hiob*,[58] Michael Heymel proposes that people who hear a lot of music through technological sound systems never learn to express themselves adequately. They also hear too much music, which is merely a source of diversion, and seldom actively listen to it. Indeed, many treat music with extreme indifference. Who among us has not thought, for instance, that they should turn on the radio in their automobile, only to realise that it was already on? People come to church today for whom music has become simply the wallpaper that is the background for their daily life. Silence becomes a problem. Teachers complain that sometimes a pupil must be asked to turn off his walkman in class. According to Heymel the quality of music has also changed with the quantity of consumption.

I cannot totally agree with Heymel, because his thesis is too one-sided. For instance, for much pop music, the quality has not declined, but improved. Other demands are placed on it, because other purposes must be fulfilled. A no less fundamental aspect of our contemporary musical culture is that the earlier visual/written manner in which music was presented has been replaced by direct contact with the sound of the music, and an audiovisual experience of music is inextricably linked with this. To my mind, this does not mean that presently music is something more listened to than something actively made. On the contrary, today ever more music is being made, but in a different way, and perhaps even better and more intensively than before. For young people music is a form of theatre, not only on MTV or in the disco, but also if they shut their eyes when alone in their rooms; even there, when all by

[58] M. Heymel: *Trost für Hiob* (Munich 1999) 16ff.

themselves, the hearing necessarily is linked with movement, as a result of complete concentration. Someone for whom music can mean this experiences music in a new and extremely active manner. With this, they learn to express themselves in a new manner. The encounter with music is so intense that they can not but respond physically. This also comes about because music today speaks less unilaterally through its melody or harmony, and much more through its rhythm and dynamics. Heymel ignores a great deal of reality when he suggests that technological apparatus changes music from a personal-interactive happening into a one-directional, passive hearing, in which the person delegates his or her own emotional expression to the music. A young person does not move when making or listening to music for the fun of it, but because he cannot help it. This person does not hand anything over to the music; on the contrary, the music is more powerful than he, and takes him in its grip.

Because a person participating in the celebration of liturgy brings the culture of his own time to the church, not only must this be taken seriously within the church, but it must become the basis of our musical-liturgical acting. In the long run, it will be impossible to only integrate contemporary musical culture into our liturgical tradition, for better or worse. It will play a fundamental role in our primary liturgical language, and therefore will be one of the most important expressive elements. The design of liturgical events will also be based in part on this. The often so physical language of the music and the aroused sensuality which accompanies it will make a positive contribution to the fullness of the liturgical proclamation. The total event too – which is what music has become for ever more people – in which the meaning of the sound cannot be 'heard' apart from the visual presentation and other forms of expression combined with it, is one of the greatest challenges for liturgical music.

There must be a very strong presumption that the answer to the increasingly loud demand of modern man for collective experience in religion is no longer to be found in a renewed movement of these people into the churches, but precisely in the other direction: in a movement of the churches to the people. That does not ultimately mean that we can close the church, but more that what we do in the church must be closer to the experience of people today. They must have the feeling that the church stands in the middle of their lives, and religious gatherings take modern society as the starting point for their thinking, speaking and acting.

9.2. A new conservatism?

In addition to the two lines of development in the contemporary celebration of liturgy mentioned above, today's world offers a third line which we can discern, namely that of a new conservatism. This line in turn branches in two directions. The one is that of the regeneration of the old and familiar feelings connected with liturgical music. For the rest, this does not come out of the blue, because it is only to be expected that the contemporary inclination to sentimentality and new forms of romanticism and piety will at the same time have their repercussions in liturgical music. As a second direction, one can discern a revival in old and traditional sounds, such as Gregorian song and the traditional devotional song.

The present liturgical-musical practice in Amsterdam's Dominicus Church is perhaps a striking example of the first direction. Once the standard bearer of the Amsterdam Study Group for Vernacular Liturgy with the experimental rhythms, dynamics and harmonies that went with that, at the moment this still flourishing community avails itself of a musical idiom that can be associated with traditional sacrality, particularly with regard to rhythm and dynamics, and furthermore can be characterised as romantic and imposing. This has not been deliberately sought out, but obviously people cannot escape from the present *Zeitgeist*, which in other places has led to the present Taizé liturgy which equally casts its eyes toward 'higher' things, and songs from evangelical quarters, which are characterised by their high hallelujah content. In Protestant circles the so excellent *Liedboek voor de Kerken* has in our time suddenly become old-fashioned, and in many congregations is being replaced by the *Evangelische Liedbundel*.[59]

In addition, one can detect a return to old traditions and classical musical repertories. If some years ago Gregorian was "in", in the context of the Old Music culture and the rise of a whole new branch in liturgical-musical studies, namely the semiology of Gregorian plainsong, today people are eager to hear it just because they are glad to hear it again. They know that they are backed up by official ecclesiastical documents, which in defining the purpose of music in the church fall back again on phraseology that stems from the end of the nineteenth century, such as

[59] *Evangelische Liedbundel* (Zoetermeer 1999).

the praise of God and the edification of the people.[60] A return to the old polyphonic song practice – Mozart, with orchestra – is openly suggested as the reason that those who previously left the church are now returning there on Sundays.[61] Pilgrimages, and the devotional songs connected with them, are also on the rise again.

Sooner or later the oscillation of the pendulum of the clock of liturgical life, which cannot be brought to a standstill, will undoubtedly make itself felt again. As always, this will inevitably bring with it a change in direction. When that happens, it may be our experience that the church music surrogates for the fleshpots of Egypt will finally be traded for more contemporary works, which undoubtedly will have integrated into themselves the good aspects of the odour of these fleshpots.

[60] See, for instance, the Instruction *Liturgiam autenticam* (2001), which, in no. 28, says of Gregorian song, that *cantus enim ille maxime valet ad spiritum humanum ad res supernas elevandum* (this song serves chiefly to elevate the human spirit toward higher things).

[61] See *Trouw*, a Dutch national newspaper, June 6, 2001, regarding Amsterdam's Obrechtkerk.

ON THE AUTHORS

Joseph Gelineau (b. 1920), liturgist and generally acknowledged as the godfather of sung liturgy in the language of the community. His particular interests have been in the various forms of psalmody and the design of the eucharistic prayer.

Ko Joosse (b. 1954), staff member for liturgical education at the Diocesan Pastoral Centre of the Diocese of Rotterdam. His dissertation (1991) was a documentary study on the development of the translated Roman and newly composed Dutch eucharistic prayers.

Huub Oosterhuis (b. 1933), poet and liturgist. Important creator of Dutch liturgical prose and song texts.

Paul Post (b. 1953), professor of liturgy and sacramental theology at the Tilburg Faculty of Theology, and director of the Liturgical Institute connected with the department.

Gerard Rouwhorst (b. 1951), professor of liturgical history, Catholic Theological University, Utrecht.

Niek Schuman (b. 1936), Professor of liturgical studies at the Theological University, Kampen; holder of the Special Chair in liturgical studies at the Free University, Amsterdam.

Louis van Tongeren (b. 1954), lecturer in liturgical studies, Tilburg Faculty of Theology, and connected with the Liturgical Institute.

Anton Vernooij (b. 1940) holder of the St. Gregorius Foundation Chair in Liturgical Music at the Tilburg Faculty of Theology.

INDEX OF NAMES

The integration of liturgical action into culture is an irrevocable process, based on contemporary social developments. In this process an important role is reserved for music. Music is constantly challenged to give artistic shape to liturgical texts in an adequate way. Moreover, its expressive richness is being rediscovered presently, and music itself is increasingly being experienced as a liturgical sign. Therefore it is an essential characteristic of continually self-renewing liturgical action that within it the community consciously makes more and more use of the language of the muse.

The symposium "Liturgy and the language of the muses", lectures from which are collected in this book, was devoted to the design of the most important component of the celebration of the Eucharist, the eucharistic prayer. All the lectures touch in one way or another on the consequences for our liturgical action of today's desire for a more inspired design for liturgy, and in particular for eucharistic prayer, in language and form. An effort is made to formulate a more precise answer to the question of how the essential elements of this prayer can be expressed optimally.

PEETERS-LEUVEN

PEETERS